Real. Big. Love.

Real. Big. Love.

*A Difference Maker's Guide
to Gain Greater Clarity, Energy,
and Impact for Your Cause and Life*

BY LISA WADE BERRY

UN-SETTLING BOOKS
Boulder, Colorado USA

Copyright © Lisa Wade Berry, 2018

All rights reserved. No part of this publication may be reproduced or transmitted in any form or by any means, mechanical or electronic, including photocopying or recording, or by any information storage and retrieval system, or transmitted by email without permission in writing from the author. Reviewers may quote brief passages in reviews. For permissions, contact Lisa Wade Berry at lisa@lisawadeberry.com.

Neither the author nor the publisher assumes any responsibility for errors, omissions, or contrary interpretations of the subject matter herein. Any perceived slight of any individual or organization is purely unintentional.

Brand and product names are trademarks or registered trademarks of their respective owners.

Cover Designer and Compositor: Sally Wright Day
Editing: Maggie McReynolds

Author's photo courtesy of Angie Graves

ISBN: 978-1-7328881-0-4

Thanks

"Nobody ever changed the world by being a chicken."
~ *Gia McGill*

Gia, I may have been your tutor as you learned to read, but you were my tutor as I learned more about how I wanted to show up in the world. Thank you for encouraging me to not let fear get in the way of helping people.

*"When you've got a big decision to make,
your head may tell you one thing
and your heart may tell you another,
but always listen to your gut."*
~ *Charlotte Wade*

Mom, this one is for you. No, it's not another grandbaby, it's a book baby. Enjoy! Thank you for always believing in and supporting me and cheering me on. Thank you for your big, kind, goofy heart and for belly laughs that are good for the soul. Regardless of how old I get,
I am deeply grateful to be your kid.

Contents

Introduction ix
Chapter 1: Difference Makers—Optimistic, But Exhausted 1
Chapter 2: Learning the Hard Way 8
Chapter 3: The Case for Soulful Service 16
       Part 1: REAL 24
Chapter 4: You Are Not Perfect, and That's Perfect 25
Chapter 5: What Makes Your Soul Sing? 31
Chapter 6: Soulful Strategies for Making "Real" Real 39
       Part 2: BIG 52
Chapter 7: Playing Big Rather than Settling for Small 53
Chapter 8: Put Your Whole Self In—Playing Hokey-Pokey
    with Service and Life 65
Chapter 9: Soulful Assessment to Support Big Service 71
       Part 3: LOVE 78
Chapter 10: Love Them Where They Are, Mess and All 79
Chapter 11: Love You Where You Are, Mess and All 87
Chapter 12: Soulful Self-Care Strategies for Bringing the Love 99
       Part 4: ACTION 118
Chapter 13: Regularly Bring Real. Big. Love. to Your Life and Service 119
Chapter 14: Obstacles to Serving and Living with Real. Big. Love 130
Conclusion 139
Resources 142
Acknowledgements 143
About the Author 145
Thank You 147

Introduction

I want to make a positive difference in the world. And, since you are reading this book, I'll guess that you do too.

We're Difference Makers, and it's clear the world needs us. Difference Makers not only want to serve a cause, but also to know that we make a meaningful contribution. We long to see the investment of our time, energy, and passion pay off—not necessarily for us, but for the people, the cause, the world we seek to uplift.

Our difference-making might be for a nonprofit or advocacy group, in our own families, in government, for a kids' team or club, in a community, purely as a solo volunteer, or in a number of other ways that we put ourselves into improving conditions that matter to us.

Wherever and however we choose to make a difference, our challenge is to balance our service with the rest of our lives. Trying to juggle all our responsibilities and to switch between the different hats we wear can be exhausting, frustrating, and overwhelming. But because we are inspired by a passion, a commitment to an ideal, or an outcome bigger than ourselves, we keep marching forward, buoyed by the belief that we can make things better.

In any direction we look, there are opportunities to be of service. In fact, all the unmet needs of the world can feel oppressive to those of us who are genuinely motivated to leave the planet in better shape than we found it. There's a lot to do, and not enough people or resources committed to doing it, which can lead many Difference Makers to feel stressed out, worn out, and swamped by the sheer magnitude of need.

For more than two decades, I've had the honor to work with Difference Makers at the local, state, regional, and national levels. I've seen their contributions, witnessed their passions, offered a shoulder during their heartbreaks, and celebrated their wins. I have been inspired by their determination, and also concerned by the lack of sleep, the long hours, the inadequate or non-existent pay, the political frustration, and the inconsistent support.

My career has spanned a broad swath of the nonprofit and public service world. From working in the smallest of local nonprofits to the US Congress, I've been motivated by the hope of making a difference, of contributing to something greater than myself.

At each turn, I got worn out. I saw my colleagues grow exhausted or weighed down with responsibility . It's not that we didn't have the skills or the smarts to get the job done. It's that the need or the cause could be so big, and with so many other things going on in life, making progress often felt like a Sisyphean task.

Like me, and like you, many of us who genuinely care find ourselves burned out and frustrated. It's not that we become apathetic. It's that we simply don't have the energy and the motivation to care about everything all at once in our professional, personal, and service worlds.

Or we feel compelled to step up our efforts even more, to give more of ourselves, and to make a bigger difference, even when we have no idea where to find the energy or hours in the day to do so.

We may even worry that nothing we do makes a damn bit of difference anyway.

I get it. I've had all these feelings. I've experienced the frustrations. I've tried to make things better. I've tried to make me better. I've been motivated and then deflated, energized then exhausted, optimistic then overwhelmed—sometimes all in the same day.

Ultimately, I found my way of being of service unsustainable. I was worn out. Burning the candle at both ends was hurting me, doing no favors for my family, and guaranteeing that I was not bringing my best self into my service.

So I grew determined to do it differently. I shifted to an approach that I now call Soulful Service and identified three qualities that helped me—and can help you—make a bigger, more meaningful, and more soulful difference in your service and in your life.

Those three qualities? Real. Big. Love.

That's how this book came to be. Together in the following pages, we'll explore the power of authenticity, of you showing up just exactly as you are, warts and all, to be of greatest service to others. We will dive into the importance of being willing to play big—either through bolder, more courageous action, or through small, regular acts, done with remarkable consistency. We will also embrace the need for love-based service, the kind of service that honors others where they are, and also supports and uplifts you where you are.

When we serve with Real. Big. Love., we make a more positive, meaningful contribution, and feel more energized and fulfilled in doing so.

My hope is that, through this book, I can help you discover a more direct path, one where you can make your biggest difference in the world by showing up and serving from a place of clarity and fullness, rather than confusion and depletion.

If you would like to make a bigger, more meaningful difference in the world and still love and enjoy your life, then please read on.

Chapter 1

Difference Makers— Optimistic, But Exhausted

Kris is a Difference Maker.

She also is a mom of three kids under 12, wife to a busy spouse who often travels for work, an accountant for a small community development nonprofit, a volunteer at a local animal shelter, a daughter responsible for the care of an increasingly frail parent, a Sunday school teacher, a political precinct captain, and the Tuesday and Thursday carpool captain taking neighborhood kids to school and from after-school activities.

For the most part, Kris manages her family, her profession, her schedule, and her responsibilities with relative ease and grace. Then there are times when a kid gets sick, the car won't start, there's a big deadline at work, Mom is in the hospital, or something else comes out of the blue that knocks her off her game and causes some of the carefully juggled balls to crash to the ground.

Kris gets frustrated, even cranky. She's worn out and needs more sleep, but pushes through to get more done instead, which exacerbates her frustration. Her kids notice, and so does her spouse. Some days she knows she's just going through the motions at work, without her usual focus and effectiveness.

In general, Kris wants to be fully present for those she serves, and she wants to be as effective as possible. But today, she really just wants a nap, and pizza would be nice.

Kris worries that taking time out to get some rest or look out for her own needs would be selfish. She has a family and a community to care for. She juggles everything but her own needs, and it catches up with her. The annual trip to the doctor becomes a thing to dread, with lectures about increasing weight, high blood pressure, and why eight hours of sleep a night is essential. (Kris always rolled her eyes at that one....)

"Yeah, yeah, yeah—lose weight, de-stress, sleep. Got it."

She even has good intentions. But one look at her to-do list makes these intentions fly out the mini-van window.

By choosing not to make herself a priority, her service to others becomes strained and unsustainable.

Can you relate?

I sure can.

You believe in trying to make the world a better place, but the effort is leaving you feeling overwhelmed, exhausted, or worried that no matter what you do, it's not enough. And no wonder. Our world, our communities, our causes, and our families are in deep need of people who care, people just like you, doing what you can to make a positive contribution, to empower others and to leave your corner of the world better. Without you and other people like you, I can't even imagine the state in which we would find our lives, our country, or our planet.

But even as you seek to make that difference, you find yourself juggling your commitments to your career, to the causes you care about, to your family and friends, and to all the other organizations to which you belong. The pressures and expectations can feel overpowering. You often feel stretched thin, even raw. It's like you're spinning plates in the air, and one misstep can send them careening in different directions before crashing to the ground.

You've wondered how to bring more balance to your life. Maybe you've even gone to a workshop or participated in a wellness program. Still, you find yourself juggling more than is comfortable. How can you make a difference and still enjoy your life?

In her book *Take Time for Your Life,* Cheryl Richardson draws awareness to obstacles that prevent us from living a life we love. These include:

- Thinking "selfish" is a dirty word
- Scheduling that doesn't reflect our priorities
- Feeling drained by people, places, and things
- Feeling trapped by money
- Using adrenaline as our main source of fuel
- Lacking a supportive community in our life
- Focusing little, if at all, on our spiritual well-being

I'm guessing a couple of these feel familiar for you. When I first read the book more than 15 years ago, these obstacles served as a wake-up call for me to get out of my own way and get on with the business of intentionally creating a life I actually enjoyed.

In the process, I found that, for those of us involved in nonprofit, volunteer, or service work, some of these obstacles can be even more pronounced. We may be passionate about our causes, and yet worn out in our lives. We prioritize making a difference for others, even when it results in sacrificing our own well-being in the process.

I once attended a workshop in which we were asked to think about and write down things we were passionate about. After completing that assignment, we were asked to write down the things that break our hearts. Every person in the room found that these two were opposite sides of the same coin. The animal lover was deeply saddened and angered by animal abuse. The child advocate was heartbroken by child endangerment and neglect. For Difference Makers, this can result in both incredibly satisfying highs and frustrating or heart-breaking lows during our service.

Statistics show that across the board employee burnout rates are on the rise, with the rate of burnout being highest among helping professions. Research on the broad topic of what I'll call "Difference Maker Burnout" is fairly limited, focusing on specific careers or workplace settings. Even less studied is the impact of burnout on volunteers (whether caregivers or cause advocates) or those who are working on multiple fronts—including at home—to make a positive difference.

In these instances, with low or no compensation and other responsibilities to juggle, the effects can be even more stressful. Volunteers who seek to balance service with family, career, and a host of other obligations can quickly feel the bite of the "I'm too busy for this volunteer business" bug and bow out. Or they may face some of the challenging symptoms of burnout, like exhaustion, frustration, changes in sleep or appetite, moodiness, irritability, relationship challenges, increased stress, or myriad physical and emotional health problems.

Across the nation, we face a dual-edged challenge that can increase the frustration for Difference Makers. Many public service programs are experiencing steep funding cuts at the local, state, and federal levels, yet the need for the services is on the rise. We have more people needing services and fewer resources to provide those services. Sound familiar?

Unfortunately, this reality causes organizations to heap more work on paid staff or to rely more on unpaid volunteers to fulfill program requirements. Those of us in service-related organizations feel the squeeze and want to do our part to meet the need. This can lead to heightened stress and anxiety for people who want to do a good job yet struggle to breathe under the mountain of increased needs and responsibilities.

Here's the truth: we give of ourselves to causes that matter to us. We feel a connection. We are passionate about making a difference. We don't want to let people down. We may even be encouraged to shoulder more because our clients, students, and causes need us now more than ever.

Do you feel guilty at the thought of letting anyone down? You're far from alone. You know there's a need, and you try to handle it all without ever needing to say "Uncle."

I get it. So, too, do many of the people I interviewed and surveyed for this book. While the folks I talked with most often said that they are optimistic and motivated about their efforts to make a difference, the vast majority also said they often felt overwhelmed, exhausted, and like they were struggling.

Optimistic, yet overwhelmed.

Motivated, yet exhausted.

Feels familiar, doesn't it?

Ironically, when Difference Makers are stretched thin, they often don't ask for help. You know how it goes. You tell yourself that the people you serve are so much worse off than you are that you can't possibly have a right to complain. Or that the cause you care about is too important for you to take a breather. Or that your family needs you, and you can't let them down.

You tell yourself you are the helper, not the one who needs help. So you juggle. That's what Difference Makers do. We keep all those balls in the air, all those plates spinning. And, in doing so, we often ignore our own needs so that we can focus on the needs of others.

Now, this isn't martyrdom stuff I'm referring to here. I know you're not looking for sympathy or admiration for being worn out through your service. Quite the contrary. You stay silent about your own needs because you don't want to bother or impose upon anyone else. It's not about any potential perceived glory. It's about making a Real, positive difference for others.

You may not even recognize the toll this approach takes on your physical, mental, emotional, and even spiritual health until the symptoms are too obvious to ignore.

MaryAnne loved her work as a home-based special education instructor. She would travel from home to home, working with 25–30 students and their families in the rural south. She was buoyed by the small gains she might see in the students and the progress made by many of the families to better manage the students' diagnoses and prognoses. MaryAnne loved this job and found it incredibly rewarding.

Then, the medically fragile children started dying.

After six months of being gutted by watching the kids she cared about die and the families she'd grown close to in such grief, MaryAnne had to leave.

"I sort of lost it. I needed a break," she remembers.

MaryAnne's grief is understandable. Folks who pursue degrees and professions in social work or counseling are warned to protect themselves from ominous sounding potential side effects of service like compassion fatigue, countertransference, and vicarious trauma. These are all fancy terms that point to how we as Difference Makers can become emotionally triggered by the work we do.

While counselors and social workers might be trained to look out for, prevent, or remedy these challenges, most of us are not.

Another side effect of service that interests me, yet doesn't get widespread attention, is the effect of service on our overall energy—both the quantity and quality of energy we experience. At its core, service is an energy exchange. As a Difference Maker, it's important that you are aware of and responsible for both the energy you are putting out into the world and also the energy you are accepting into *your world*.

Many cause-oriented Difference Makers are also empathetic, some even empathic. This means that we can be like sponges, unintentionally soaking up the energy around us and especially the energy of those we serve. If this energy is joyous, positive, and uplifting, that's fantastic. Often though, the work we do may include trauma, drama, negativity, and heartbreak. We can absorb this energy too and carry it into the rest of our lives where it can begin to affect our own attitude, health, relationships, and well-being.

Another challenge is that of the energy vampire. These are the people or situations that seem to suck the life force right out of us. You know, the ones where you feel totally drained after interacting with them? It's exhausting and unsustainable.

For both Kris and MaryAnne, the challenging effects of their own difference-making caught up with them. But your service doesn't need to go that way.

The world needs you, and all Difference Makers, to keep caring, to keep taking action. Rather than getting easier, the stakes are getting higher. The world is in deep need of compassionate, energized, action-oriented people who are willing and able to help improve their corner of the world, advocate for their cause, and offer a hand to struggling brothers and sisters—over the long haul.

The world needs you. Yes, you. And, you need you.

How are you going to make a difference in the world and still enjoy your life?

Let's find out together.

CHAPTER 2

Learning the Hard Way

In one way or another, my entire career has focused on some aspect of empowering positive change. The only "corporate" job I've ever had, beyond scooping ice cream or delivering pizza in my youth, was starting my own company (Empower Change, Inc.) to offer consulting and coaching services to organizations, communities, and individuals dedicated to improving their corner of the world.

The seed of service was planted early in my life, albeit unintentionally.

It was Christmas Eve morning. Mom loaded a very reluctant preteen me into the car to make the short trek across town to the local Elks Lodge. Although the morning was grey and dreary outside, the attitude inside the lodge was light and festive as we joined a group to assemble Christmas boxes to deliver to families in need.

I helped stuff the turkeys and hams, mashed potato flakes, and canned goods into the boxes, along with toys and books in boxes going to families with kids.

Christmas was always a big, happy occasion in my family. Nothing extravagant, mind you, with a single mom raising two kids without child support, we didn't do fancy. The holidays centered around family togetherness and way too much food, and there were always presents to unwrap.

On this Christmas Eve, my young mind was opened to the fact that, for many people, the holiday experience is very different. Big meals and gifts aren't a certainty.

When it was time to deliver the boxes, I wanted to go. Mom thought nothing of loading me up in the middle of a truck bench seat with two grown men we didn't know and sending me to the tiny town of Picher, OK, to hand out the Christmas goodies.

While the town of Picher has since been decommissioned due to the hazardous contamination from an abandoned lead and zinc mine, the memory of this morning in this small town set the course for my interest in Difference Making.

As we took the boxes up to the houses and mobile homes, I was struck by the reactions of the recipients. Gratitude from the adults. Utter excitement from the kids upon seeing that they would get a Christmas present after all. Some people seemed a bit embarrassed that they needed the help. Others shared how this gift from the community was the one good thing about their holiday.

We come to service in different ways and for different reasons. I look back to that experience and see that the seed of service was planted in me on that day, a seed that would eventually grow into a passion and a career path.

But this path hasn't been clear and smooth.

My first experience working for a cause was in college when I interned for the Muscular Dystrophy Association in Kansas City. The highlight was staffing the summer camp for kids afflicted with the disease. The smiles, the excitement, the laughter, and the confidence the kids showed while being among their peers was infectious. If I could help make their lives even a touch better during that week, I knew my time there mattered.

After college, my attention turned to politics and working to make a difference through campaigns, and the media and policy route, with nonprofits and elected officials.

Living and working in the Washington, D.C. area for nearly

12 years was fascinating, and also exhausting. Between a stint doing public affairs for the fuel-focused agency of the Department of Defense, strategic communication regarding environmental politics at the League of Conservation Voters, on Capitol Hill, and for a regional adult literacy nonprofit, I had the chance to engage in a variety of positions designed to promote the general welfare and serve the public.

The pace, the long hours, the big personalities, and the partisanship all converged to feel both exhilarating and suffocating at the same time.

Some colleagues thrived in that environment. For others, it seemed that the stress and high demands could cause them to unravel at any moment.

While serving as Communication Director for a US Senator, I hit my limit. The long hours, stress, and politics were one thing, but the terror attacks of 9-11 and the subsequent Anthrax scare made me feel like my internal walls were caving in. Serious emotional claustrophobia. My attempts to look after my own well-being were inconsistent and fell dangerously short.

I needed out.

It was a Friday in July. The weekend before my 30th birthday. I needed to breathe. Big sky and big nature would help too. Rather than make local plans to take a hike or do something sensible, I scoured the internet and found dude ranches out west that were hiring. I had two phone interviews on Saturday that resulted in two job offers, one at a ranch in Wyoming and one in Montana. Scrubbing toilets and mucking horse stalls for the rest of the tourist season seemed like just the reset I needed.

On Monday, I attempted to resign from my position. I left messages for my boss, but, perpetually busy, he didn't call back.

On Tuesday, I learned I was pregnant with my one-and-only daughter.

Needless to say, I stayed at my job, and my season cleaning stalls and toilets at a dude ranch hasn't happened yet.

I'll never know if it was the stress, the pregnancy hormones, or something else that made me want to run. I do know that if I had been listening to my body and even to the whispers of my soul, I could have handled my feelings of claustrophobia with a bit more grace and self-compassion.

In the later stages of my pregnancy, my blood pressure shot up and the doctors encouraged bed rest. I ignored them, of course. I had important work to do, and people were counting on me. That was until the Senate nurse panicked at a high blood pressure reading and called my doctor, who then threatened to call my boss and force me to go home if I didn't do it on my own.

My boss was incredibly understanding, and the last month of my pregnancy I worked from home. The sky didn't fall. Life went on. My dear friend in the office filled in during my absence, which offered a perfect transition for and after maternity leave.

I got caught up in the crazy-making of trying to make a difference. That was my choice, not something that was forced upon me. But it nearly put both my health and my unborn daughter's health in serious jeopardy.

Later, I decided to depart Capitol Hill in order to spend more than 45 waking minutes a day with my daughter. I launched a home-based consulting practice to help clients garner attention for their causes and to promote their message to a broader audience. During this time, I also volunteered as an adult literacy tutor and worked part-time and consulted for the local literacy council.

Helping adults learn to read lit me up from the inside. Directly empowering others to gain new skills and confidence, for me, was juicy, soul-affirming stuff.

My family eventually moved back to Oklahoma, so my then-husband could pursue his political ambitions.

Surely leaving the hectic pace of D.C. and finding big sky again would make the claustrophobic feelings and stress disappear, right?

Not exactly.

It turns out, D.C. wasn't the problem. I was. We Difference Makers can have unhealthy standards and unrealistic expectations for ourselves regardless of where we might live or work.

I quickly found myself overweight, exhausted, unhappily married, and striving to help empower the dreams of others while putting my own goals on hold.

If I could only serve more, I thought, I'd feel better. If I could keep myself busy making a difference for others, then the many differences that needed to be made in my own life wouldn't seem so stark. Plus, others have it worse off than I do. How can I complain about being unhappy when I have it pretty good in comparison?

Utter crap. All of it. It felt so real at the time. Oh, I'm sure I felt quite magnanimous while volunteering time for boards and causes, but I was so over-extended and stressed that I wasn't fully showing up for any of it.

I was trapped in three modes of unhelpful thinking:
1. I thought that spending time in service would fix or at least add a shinier finish to an unfulfilling life.
2. I was convinced that time spent on making me healthier or happier or saner was selfish. There were dishes to do, school lunches to make, family outings to orchestrate, work to do, people to serve, and nonprofit responsibilities to attend to. Any free time I had should have been invested in others, in family, in work, in service.
3. I thought showing up was enough. I didn't recognize that I was doing no one any favors by serving while empty. Helping transform situations takes energy, energy that, without copious amounts of caffeine, I simply did not have at the time.

I read books, a lot of books, mainly the self-help variety, each of them espousing their version of what I "should" be doing in my life. I created goals. Often, they were the same goals, made year after year and never attained.

Shortly after moving back to Oklahoma, I had the chance to serve as the founding executive director of a nonprofit resource center. In this capacity, I worked alongside other Difference Makers who were passionate about their causes. They, too, were often excited, yet exhausted; motivated, yet often overwhelmed. While nonprofit training programs tend to focus on capacity-building for the organization—things like fundraising, grant writing, volunteer recruitment, and program development—emphasis on the well-being, energy, and vitality of the Difference Makers implementing the programs was missing.

I knew that the organizations and programs could only be as effective as the people leading them.

With that understanding, I became certified as an organizational and life coach and a nonprofit consultant. When the opportunity came about to lead a community wellness initiative, I knew that the "eat better, move more, be tobacco-free" mantra was about more than just physical health, and could benefit emotional and mental well-being too.

I knew the things I needed to do to feel better physically, emotionally, and mentally. I encouraged others to take positive action to support their well-being. Still, I didn't walk the talk with any long-term consistency.

After getting divorced, I was still consulting and also took a "safe" job with benefits directing a scholarship and wellness program and also teaching classes at a local community college. As the state faced budget shortages and funding for higher education was slashed, my job description burgeoned with responsibilities of others who'd departed the organization and had not been replaced due to budget shortfalls. Grant writing, economic development, coordinating Americans with Disabilities Act accommodations for students, and overseeing a collaborative program to make college classes available to incarcerated students inside two local state prisons were added to my plate.

The "safe" job wasn't so safe after all. I felt like I was drinking from a fire hose and drowning in the process. The stress got to me. To deal with it, I ate. My weight hit a non-pregnancy high, and my blood pressure skyrocketed. Although I tried to talk with the administration, they didn't have many options to lighten the load.

With the support and encouragement of my new husband, I eventually left the staff position, but continued adjunct teaching. I particularly enjoyed teaching classes inside the prisons where I felt like I could make the biggest difference.

I returned to my consulting and coaching practice with a renewed hope of empowering others: to help organizations, communities, and individuals alike gain clarity on the path forward and more effectively strive toward making their missions or their goals manifest in the world.

Throughout the struggles, that seed desire to make a difference that was planted as a young girl was still there, but by not regularly tending to myself, I let it get buried in heaviness rather than allowing it to truly bloom.

My focus continued to be external. The mindset of, "How can I improve things out there?" kept me from focusing on the real work that needed to happen "in here."

Then the phrase from Gandhi smacked me in the heart and changed the way I look at service. "Be the change you wish to see in the world."

I finally realized that to contribute fully in the world, to make my unique difference, I had to start with myself. I needed to consider what really lights me up and then to make *me* a priority in my own life. I no longer had the luxury of telling myself that it was selfish, or that I didn't have enough time. I needed to tend my inner garden regularly if I was going to show up and make the difference my family and community needed me to make.

And I needed support. Asking for and receiving help is not a sign of weakness, but rather a sign of commitment. Independent to a fault, this was (and sometimes still is) a remarkably difficult lesson for this girl who thought she could do it all on her own.

I took the long, winding, circuitous route to figure this out. I invested decades in detours, backtracks, and lessons learned and then quickly forgotten, only to be learned again. In writing this book, my hope is to help your path to Soulful Service be more direct and enjoyable.

The recent political shifts in the nation also provided impetus for writing this book now. Many Difference Makers feel that the causes we care about are at risk, even under siege. We see a need for increased compassion and support for others at a time when policies and politics feel more divisive and alienating.

I've talked to Difference Makers who are fired up to push full-tilt until they see the changes they want, and risk burning out in the process. I've talked to others who feel shell-shocked by the division they see in the news and the venom in their social media feeds and are retreating in order to save their sanity.

I believe there's another way.

Now more than ever, I feel compelled to support progressive Difference Makers in their quest to be effective, uplifting, and sustainable in their efforts. I have finally learned that, through the guiding principles of Real. Big. Love. and the art of Soulful Service, we can make an inspired, meaningful difference while bringing more clarity, energy, and balance to our lives too.

I took a lot of detours and backtracks to figure it out. But, now I'm excited to light a more direct path for others. This is how my seed of service finally blooms.

Chapter 3

The Case for Soulful Service

Is the idea of "selfless" service potentially a disservice? Is it actually possible to give to others and not get anything back in return? Is it possible that in taking care of yourself you can be of even greater service to others?

Hmmm...

Typically, we have some reason we want to get involved or invest our time, energy, and resources into a cause. We have a reason to care. Making a difference will in some way help others and also help us too.

Here's a little secret: It is totally okay to derive some sense of satisfaction or fulfilled purpose or warm fuzzy from serving. It's not selfish. It's the juice that keeps us going.

Granted, some people get into service for what appear to be warped reasons. And, some people dedicate so much of themselves to service that they ultimately flame out.

I believe a model that I call Soulful Service allows you to make a more meaningful difference with and for those you serve while actually giving you more clarity, energy, and joy in your service and your life.

The Downside of Selfless Service

Ah, selfless service. It's the stuff of which saints are made, right? This is the ideal to which many of us aspire. "Service Above Self" (the

Rotary Club motto) is noble. "Selfless service" is even one of the seven core values of the Army.

The idea is to serve others or causes without expectation of reciprocity or reward. In fact, in many helping-type fields, direct reciprocity or expectation can even be considered unethical or a violation of professional standards. To be more concerned about uplifting and supporting others than with personal gain is a noble calling.

However, there's a shady side of selfless service.

The British Dictionary defines selfless as "having little concern for one's own interests." Merriam-Webster defines it as "having or showing great concern for other people and little or no concern for yourself."

Thinking more about selfless service, I'm left scratching my head and feeling conflicted. Serving a cause outside ourselves with no expectation for return or reward, but to sincerely meet the needs of others—that is a beautiful thing, worth striving toward. But it worries me when the idea of selfless service becomes perverted to mean that we are selfish if we also take care of our needs.

Having or showing great concern for other people (or animals, or the planet, or beliefs, etc.) and little or no concern for yourself.

You're smart. You know where I'm going with this.

Caring for others and the greater good without regard for your own well-being can be counterproductive, both for yourself and for those you serve. The selfless service model might even allow you to feel completely justified in placing a lower value on your own needs or cause you to feel guilty for making your own well-being a priority.

Let's rethink this.

First, if we honestly choose to have little or no concern for ourselves, then we really aren't much good to others. Our light dims. Our energy wanes. We aren't able to show up as healthy, vital, full people with the energy and desire to make a difference over the long haul.

And, face it, none of our causes are quick fixes. If they were, then we would not be needed. Instead, this business of change—personal, cultural, societal—takes a marathon, not a sprint, of commitment. If we believe that taking care of ourselves is selfish or against the tenets of selfless service, then we are denying our cause the best of ourselves, and our long-term commitment.

Secondly, why would we do what we do, if not for the hope of some kind of progress for the cause? We want to see people grow and succeed. We want to see animals in safe, loving homes. We want to see the earth well-cared for. We want to see our neighborhoods safer, our schools supported, and our groups thriving. We want to see people held in care and compassion as they face health challenges or impending death. We want to see people free of that which holds them back, so they may thrive in the world. We are propelled by the hope that our involvement can make a difference.

We hope, with our encouragement, others will take the steps to realize progress for themselves. Helpful, empowering aims are necessary to build resilience and confidence in others. When we don't feel progress is being made toward those aims, we can get discouraged, be at greater risk of burnout, or feel personally frustrated and like our service is for naught.

It's healthy to see that our engagement actually makes a difference—both for us and for those whom we serve. Again, that's fuel to keep us going.

Finally, it's impossible to make a difference and not derive some benefit in return. I'm a big fan of the Prayer of St. Francis. I believe in the line, "It is in giving that we receive." As people committed to service, we know this to be true.

Whether cleaning up our community improves quality of life for our family, adopting a pet brings unconditional love into our home, or making a meaningful connection uplifts both parties, we are somehow boosted by our commitment. The Universe is pretty cool in that way. It becomes a self-reinforcing cycle of giving and receiving of goodness. Sure, the goodness we get back is often not the same as what we gave, but we receive nonetheless.

When I am teaching—whether on a college campus, in a prison, or through my own workshops and retreats—my intention is always to share information and ideas in a way that empowers others. When I go in with this approach, I am consistently amazed at how much I learn and grow in the process. That's the beautiful gift of service: When you seek to uplift others, you can't help but be uplifted yourself.

There's nothing selfish about deriving some inherent joy from service. It fills your energy tanks so you can keep going. There is danger, though, in consistently putting your needs last while you strive to serve the needs of others first. This is a recipe for exhaustion, burnout, and worse.

During her 13 years as a child protection worker, Fiona struggled to balance the needs of the families she served, her love of her job, and her own well-being.

"I was held hostage, threatened, propositioned, assaulted, and called every name under the sun, and I even attended a funeral or two," she explains. "But I loved my job. I was good at it. I had finally found something that I loved doing. It fulfilled me, even with all the crap that happened, all of the tragic moments that I witnessed."

She didn't realize, though, the toll the job was taking on her mental and physical health.

"What I didn't know was that I was sinking into a depression," she says. "After 13 years on the job, 13 years of being called a liar on a daily basis, 13 years of children being afraid of me, 13 years of watching families struggle to make changes—there was really nothing I could do."

Fiona's job required her to tell families they needed to change, but the organization she worked for didn't offer the resources and services families needed to be successful in making those lasting changes.

"I started to leave for appointments early because I knew I needed to have a nap before I got there," remembers Fiona. "I started to get angry for no apparent reason, even my family questioned what was happening. I was afraid that if I spoke up, my clients would be hurt, I would get into trouble, that I would lose my job. So I sucked it up, put on a brave face, and went to work every day. What I didn't know was that I was losing myself and becoming someone I didn't like very much."

Fiona took an important step and went to see a doctor. She was diagnosed with depression and prescribed medication, and she quickly started therapy. Ultimately, she realized that the service she loved providing, where she felt she made a difference, was unsustainable. For her own health and sanity, she made the difficult decision to resign.

Fiona shifted her focus away from Selfless Service and toward more nourishing Soulful Service. She insists on making her own well-being a priority so she can show up for others in a bigger, more authentic way. Now, she has reclaimed her voice and tells her story on stage to urge other caregivers and service providers to not deny their own needs while seeing to the needs of others. She even became a speaking coach and the host of momondays Niagara, a local program to empower others to tell their story on stage to a local, supportive audience.

Making the Shift to Soulful Service

What if, in taking care of yourself and your own needs in life, you are able to serve others and your cause even better?

What if, when you fill yourself up with love, energy, well-being, purpose, and support, you are then able to make a greater contribution? What if, by ignoring your own needs, you are actually letting other people down?

What if self-denial is the most selfish thing we can do for our service? Ouch.

Yep. Been there, done that.

We've probably all heard the tired analogy of how, when in an airplane and the cabin pressure changes, we should put our own oxygen mask on first before helping others. The idea of course is that we are of little good to anyone else if we are incoherent from oxygen deprivation...or worse.

How about a different visual to help make the point? Think back to the "I'm a Little Teapot" song from our youth. Consider that you are the teapot. You may not be short or stout, but you are pouring out your brand of service to benefit others.

Now, what if you keep pouring from your little teapot? And then you pour some more? Someone else needs tea, you better pour more. Just keep pouring, just keep pouring.... Eventually, of course, the teapot runs dry. It's empty. There's nothing left to serve.

You are the teapot. You are responsible for filling yourself up, and refilling yourself regularly, so you can continue to have something worthwhile to offer.

I tend to think in terms of energy. The teapot analogy could just as easily be about fuel in your car. Running on fumes is dangerous and likely to leave you stranded. Putting poor quality fuel in the system leads to crappy performance.

How are you filling yourself up? In nourishing ways that help drive and support your service or are you perpetually running on empty, ignoring the low fuel gauge and just praying you can get through the next thing before stalling out?

That's why I'd like to shift our framework from selfless service to Soulful Service.

Soulful Service is aligned with our strengths and passions (Real), it is bold (Big), it is driven by Love, and it is sustainable. Throughout the following four parts of the book, we dive into each of these in greater depth, exploring exactly how they apply to you and raise the potential of your Soulful Service.

In Soulful Service, we bring our full selves, our balanced selves, our happy selves, our whole selves to our service. We fill ourselves up so that we are not already depleted when we seek to offer help to a program, a cause, and especially to people. We serve from the overflow of our own fullness.

If you are the teapot or the car, you are responsible, not only for filling yourself up, but also for the quality of the contents with which you fill ourselves. Are you filling up with murky, polluted thoughts and energy that is toxic, both to you and those you serve? Or are you filling up with nourishing, enriching, uplifting energy that is a blessing to yourself and those around you?

Esther Hicks once wrote, "The greatest gift you can ever give another person is your own happiness." Whoa! Being happy isn't selfish, it's a gift to both ourselves and others.

Now we're talking!

Trust me when I say that your friends and family will appreciate your happiness, and so will the causes and people you serve.

Fiona's journey back to herself wasn't a straight line. In the year after she resigned. she lost her mom and her precious dog, her husband became ill, and she welcomed a grandson into the world. Through the rollercoaster, and continued unemployment, she felt herself slipping away again.

Fiona's turning point toward Soulful Service came in a phone call in which her coach asked what she was doing, why she wasn't looking after herself, and why she wasn't standing in her light.

"That one phone call led me to start on a journey of self-discovery and self-help that has changed me. I am strong, I am confident, I live in the light again, and I have my voice back.

I started to believe in myself," she explains.

"I have learned that my voice can help others. You see, all of those years working as a social worker took away my voice. I was afraid to use it. I had lost my ability to care about my work, and because of all of this, I lost the ability to stand up for myself and my clients. When I look back, I wish I would have had someone who could have helped me find my voice to take back my power."

Through Soulful Service, you are better able to stand in your power, exercise your voice, feel supported, and better serve others. To do that, you must attend to your own needs.

Throughout this book, we will explore a buffet of proactive strategies that you can pick and choose from to keep your teapot or your fuel tank full. I'll ask you to think about what makes you tick, where you invest your energy, the roles you play in life. We'll explore those places where you may be playing small, and why. And, by the end of the book, you'll have a framework for looking out for you so that you can serve others with greater energy, clarity, balance, and impact. At the end of each chapter, you'll be asked to apply the Soulful Service concepts to how you show up in service and in life.

I've identified Eight Spheres of Soulful Self-Care that can help you attend to your own needs and serve from a place of fullness, and to actually enjoy your life more when you are not serving others, too. The suggestions offered for each of the eight spheres are not elaborate, time-sucking things to add to your already overflowing plate, but rather quick, easy, and inexpensive ways to intentionally integrate care for yourself into your life so that you can more completely share your gifts with others. Think of them as Difference Maker hacks that can support you in serving your cause, your family, or your community with greater energy and results.

The Eight Spheres of Soulful Self-Care offer suggestions and ideas to nurture, support, or unleash more potential through our body, mind, heart, spirit, energy, voice, resources, and community. They provide a starting place for us to rethink and recreate our own way of Soulful Service that benefits both those we serve, and ourselves.

Instead of waiting until your teapot "shouts," you learn to invest in your own well-being and to choose Soulful Service. In this way, you keep your teapot filled so that you may pour the best of yourself into your service and the world.

*Authenticity is the daily practice of letting go
of who we think we're supposed to be
and embracing who we are.*

~ Brené Brown

Part 1: REAL

INFUSING REAL INTO SOULFUL SERVICE:

- Soulful Service aligns with your personal, inherent strengths. It is a vehicle for you to bring your gifts into the world.

- Soulful Service brings that which makes your soul sing alive in how you show up for your cause.

- Soulful Service asks you to be you, recognizing that only through authenticity can Real, meaningful progress be made.

- Soulful Service asks you to graciously allow those you serve to also be themselves as the starting point for your work together.

CHAPTER 4

You Are Not Perfect, and That's Perfect

You care. That's why you serve. And that says a lot about you. Now, let me ask one favor: Please continue to be you, completely you, amazingness, warts, and all. *That's* the you that the world needs. The Real you. The messy you. The perfectly imperfect you.

When we are in the business of serving, it's our own experiences, our own stories, our own understanding of the world that help us be effective in the difference we are trying to make. Often, it's the hardships we've faced, the mistakes we've made, our struggles and our growth, that allow us to authentically interact and engage with others. Ultimately, it's our imperfections and how we deal with challenges that make us Real. That's how other people can connect with and relate to us.

When you own your stuff—not let it define you, but rather integrate it and grow from it—you can show up as your authentic self and make a stronger connection and bigger difference through your service.

President Theodore Roosevelt had it right. "No one cares how much you know until they know how much you care." When we hide parts of ourselves, when we wall ourselves off, it's hard for others to know how much we care.

Sometimes, those we serve feel the least worthy of our care. They've faced struggles. They've faced challenges. Maybe they are learning something new. Maybe they are overcoming something old. Maybe they are struggling to be humble about receiving when their pride hurts that they need help at all.

In these instances, they don't need our judgment. They need our understanding. If they know why we care about their situation and how we understand it, then they may be more open to our service. Whether serving in a soup kitchen or an art class, those we encounter can benefit from our compassion and our authenticity.

That's not to say that you need to have been homeless to serve those on the streets, or that you need to have faced addiction to serve those seeking to become sober. It is not necessary that you've experienced the same circumstances, but it is important to realize that your own challenging experiences can help you be and be seen as more Real and caring to others.

John Cooper (Coop) is an Alcohol and Substance Abuse Counselor in an alternative high school that serves students who, for myriad reasons, are not able to succeed in a traditional high school. Coop is also a recovering addict, a fact that both motivates him to give his all and that helps his students trust that he understands what they may be going through. He connects. He is Real. He earns their trust and their respect because he shows he cares, and he's willing to discuss his less-than-sparkling past.

The students he reaches don't want another adult talking at them, preaching to them, or writing them off. They need an adult who is Real, who cares, and who believes in their ability to create a better life for themselves.

"Being real helps. Kids can smell BS a mile away. My past helps—not the fact that I had one, but what I did to get past one," says Coop. "Self-disclosure and transparency matter. When you can know your own faults and voice them, kids respond to that."

Without having lived through his struggles and then being willing to own and share them, Coop couldn't have the same connection with or impact on students. His willingness to be Real makes the difference.

I live in a region that faces higher than average poverty rates, a fact that correlates to lower educational attainment, higher incarceration and addiction rates, and other community challenges. When the community launched an effort to help people in poverty gain the skills and confidence to build their resources for success, I knew it could be a game changer.

The community trainings in the Bridges Out of Poverty program seek to increase understanding about poverty as a means to reduce judgment and misunderstanding between the economic classes. Of all the principles taught through the Bridges Out of Poverty program, I particularly appreciate this idea from Dr. James Comer, a professor of child psychiatry at Yale University: "No significant learning occurs without a significant relationship."

I've seen in my own life that I learn more, and have the opportunity for meaningful change, transformation even, when the education grows from a foundation of mutual respect and desire for mutual understanding.

Judgment impedes relationships; commonalities help strengthen them.

However, it's those commonalities that we can be most hesitant to acknowledge. Being Real can make us feel vulnerable, and that can be scary. But imagine if we think first of those we seek to serve and appreciate the vulnerability they must be experiencing to receive support or assistance. Imagine if we put our own fears of vulnerability aside and invited others to do the same.

I've witnessed the flip side of this premise too. A local organization I once belonged to hosted a monthly free meal for members of the community in need. It's a nice concept that helps fill hungry bellies on a Saturday afternoon. I volunteered several times to help prepare and serve the food and appreciated the opportunity to engage with those who came to eat. What surprised me were the snide comments of some volunteers who served sandwiches and casseroles with a side dish of judgment.

When judgment takes the place of understanding, service encounters become transactional, with no real opportunity for deeper meaning or transformation on either side. Pretentiousness and a "better than" attitude create resistance, not relationship.

In addition to being Real ourselves, we also need to give others the space and courtesy to be Real, to be who and where they are right now. Sure, they may have a desire to grow, to learn, to shift, to change in some way, and that's great. But judging them for where they are does not create a foundation for supporting them in moving toward where they would like to be.

I have the opportunity to teach college classes inside two state prisons. My students there have made mistakes. They know this. The court system has been quite clear on this fact. What they don't need from me is a constant reminder of the guilt, judgment, and shame they already feel toward themselves and their past decisions. I try to show up, be Real, and encourage them to connect with and show up from the place of their authentic, best selves.

In these classes I teach at the prisons, I have three rules: 1) Be respectful of each other and expect that I will be respectful of you; 2) No dumbassery (they "get" this one); and 3) Show up as your best self.

Best self? This isn't a concept many have considered. What is my best self? What does that look like? How does it feel?

None of them believe that it was acting from their best selves that landed them in prison.

I don't tell them what their best self is or what it "should" be. It's different for everyone. But I do get them thinking about what "best self" means for them, what that could look and feel like, and how their lives might proceed differently if they consciously acted from a place of their personal best selves.

If I have some preconceived notion of what their best self is and expect them to conform to it, that creates distance. Instead, I share that I'm a work in progress too and give them space to imagine and begin to integrate what "best self" means to them.

Another concept I share, especially during an introductory speech class I teach there, is the importance for them to know their audience and to craft and communicate their speeches based not on their own personal needs, but on the needs of the audience.

This concept applies both to speeches and to service.

When we craft our service to meet those we serve where they are, both our effort and the results are more effective. When we cater only to our own expectation or our own needs, without recognizing, understanding, or honoring where another might be or what his or her needs really are, we miss an opportunity. Although possibly more convenient, a one-size-fits-all approach to service isn't as effective.

During the speech class, we also talk about the willingness to be vulnerable, to speak from our truth and from our hearts, even when—or especially when—it's uncomfortable. As you can imagine, the thought of opening up during a speech when the audience is a room full of other convicted felons can feel more than intimidating, it can feel dangerous. However, the students quickly realize the difference in those speeches in which the speaker clearly spoke from a place of authenticity and vulnerability, and those who remained cloistered in their small comfort zone.

The difference is real when we choose to be Real.

When we can be ourselves and allow others to be themselves without all the judgment in between, beautiful things can happen. If we are judging ourselves and not being Real with who we are and what really matters to us, then it's next to impossible to allow others that courtesy.

The trick is in finding the balance—to act in integrity with who we are and also meet people where they are, especially when the two may be worlds apart. Can we honor both without judgment or the dreaded "should"? Can we honor both because we realize that our paths are different and it's those different paths that brought us right here, right to this moment of possibility? Can we honor both because that is how deeper, more meaningful service happens and that's ultimately what we really want?

As Anaïs Nin wrote, "We don't see things as they are, we see things as we are." That applies to people and to service.

SOULFUL SERVICE CONSIDERATIONS:

What parts of yourself do you hide
in your service?
Why do you feel the need to hide those parts?

Is it possible you could connect with others more effectively if you chose to own those parts of yourself rather than hide them?

What is the worst that could happen if you were Real about those parts of you?

What is the best that could happen if you were Real about those parts of you?

Is the risk of being Real worth it?

CHAPTER 5

What Makes Your Soul Sing?

You know those people you meet and instantly like? That was my experience with Hillary. We both worked at a literacy council in northern Virginia. She taught English as a Second Language to adults who were predominately illiterate in their native language. Not the easiest task. But Hillary has a smile and laugh that can electrify a room. Her desire to leave the world better than she found it becomes quickly obvious to those who hear her talk or see her interact with those she serves.

"I serve because I truly feel like if we are not here in this life to help others, then what are we here for? We can take nothing with us into the next life but how people made us feel and how we made others feel, and that's of utmost importance to me," says Hillary. "Also, being of service feels good, makes me happy, and gives me an outlet while I'm raising my children."

The desire to serve runs deep for her. It's a fundamental part of who she is and the value she chooses to offer in this life. She has experienced personal challenges, including mental health struggles, and uses those experiences as building blocks to connect with others and offer a sense of hope and compassion. And while she doesn't pretend to have it all figured out in her life, she has a strong compass and sense of direction for making choices that reflect her true nature.

What is our true nature? How do we know what really matters to us? How do we differentiate between our own wants and needs and those things that other people believe we should want and need?

"Know thyself." The ancient Greeks recognized the value in this premise. But what the hell does that really mean, and how do we go about excavating our truest inner nature?

So who are you? Really?

It was a sweltering Oklahoma day in July when I picked up my then seven-year-old daughter from a summer art camp. Despite the triple-digit heat and high humidity that made me feel like I was melting, she had a lightness and bounce to her walk, a carefree joviality that, while not unusual for her, was certainly amplified that day.

"Seeing you this happy makes me smile. Why are you so happy today?" I asked.

Her response was immediate and simple: "Mommy, doing art makes my soul sing."

Doing art makes my soul sing.

What a beautiful concept. What a precious recognition from one so young.

Her matter-of-fact response made me smile from the inside. I immediately started wondering what makes my own soul sing. What is it that I get lost in, that inspires pure joy? What makes me feel like the truest, freest, most Real version of myself?

Hmmm… I wasn't immediately sure.

This wasn't the first time I was taken off-guard by this notion.

Ten years earlier at a trade association banquet (aka an "old folks prom") in Washington, D.C., a woman I had never met before asked me a question that left me reeling and answer-less.

I was innocently returning from a trip to the restroom when I passed by her seat on my way back to my table. She grabbed my arm and pulled me close so she could look right into my eyes. I quickly knew that she had definitely taken good advantage of the open bar that evening. Then, in a cocktail-fueled slur, she asked, "What are you passionate about?"

Excuse me?

"What are you passionate about?"

I told her where I worked—an environmental nonprofit.

"I didn't ask where you work. I asked what you're passionate about."

Humpfff. I passed by and returned to my table, head spinning. How dare this slurring stranger turn my entire night upside down with this nosy question?

What *am* I passionate about? Oh shit. I could feel the anxiety pass over me in waves. You mean work and passion can be two different things? Oh shit. But I'm doing work that matters. Doesn't that count for something? Oh shit. But I graduated top of my grad school class. Oh shit.

My "oh shit" heap grew deeper, and with every question I asked myself came the sinking realization that I had no effing idea what I was passionate about. That question haunted me for years and years afterward.

What am I passionate about? What makes my soul sing?

Same question, really.

While I have no interest in shoving you into your own stinking "oh shit" heap, do you know the answer for you? What are you passionate about? What makes your soul sing? Why do you serve?

Don't worry, there's no right or wrong answer, no test to pass that gives you entrance into the next phase of your life. We can go our entire lives and never recognize what lights us up from the inside.

But would we want to?

Within the answer to this question also likely lies the key to the greatest contribution you can make on this planet, your most authentic and even magnificent path to service.

If we want to make a Real difference, a Big difference, and Love our life in the process, then aligning our service with our passion is one way to make our soul sing. That's the first invitation of the Soulful Service model.

For some, this is easy. They know without a shadow of a doubt what lights them up. Others of us may have buried the answer under years of judgment, fear, avoidance, and other aspects of the stink heap. That's not a criticism, because it's actually quite normal.

What is it for you? What makes your soul sing? What are you ridiculously good at? What makes you lose track of time? When do you feel most like you?

These questions are not rhetorical in nature. Think about them. Make this your own personal treasure hunt. What makes you tick matters.

Get your head out of the clouds. Be practical and logical. That's nice, but does it pay the bills? Nice girls don't _____. Sound familiar? These phrases are dream killers, passion stealers, attitudes that muzzle the singing of the soul.

Maybe you hear things like that from someone else. Maybe you hear it from the bully in your own brain shouting at you again. You're familiar with that voice, right? That Bully Brain seeks to keep you safe, but it can also keep you small and steal your joy in the process.

You can choose to respectfully hear all the shoulds of others and even the shoulds from your own Bully Brain, and then choose a different path. You can choose to explore, embrace, and harness your passion as your path to bring your unique brand of service and joy to the world.

To uncover and find my passion, it felt like I was going on a treasure hunt of sorts, complete with circuitous routes, plenty of backtracking, and a broken compass. But finding the treasure was worth it, and it helped me contribute in a more meaningful and motivating way for others.

Getting Real

Understanding what makes your soul sing, or knowing your deep, inner *why*, is like having your life's compass pointed toward how you can make your biggest difference and feel the most joy in the process. It is your inner North Star that points the way toward your version of meaningful service and offering your most authentic Inner Spark to the world.

What is your why? Why do you serve?

When I coach clients, we jump in with a number of questions designed to pull the Real right out of them. Several of the questions and suggestions are included below. Break out a journal and get ready to go on a little treasure hunt—the treasure being you! Or, better yet, download the Real. Big. Love. Workbook by visiting this link: www.lisawadeberry.com/RBL_Workbook.

Exploration

"Don't ask yourself what the world needs. Ask yourself what makes you come alive, and then go do that. Because what the world needs is people who have come alive." Howard Thurman taps into such an important concept with these words.

When we know what lights us up on the inside, when we know what fans the flame of our Inner Spark, *that* is the gift we most need to share with the world through our service. When you align your service with your Inner Spark, it becomes inspired and soulful.

To find that, let's first differentiate the WooHoo! from the HoHum in your life. Take a couple of minutes to brainstorm and write out what makes you feel most Real, most you, most alive, most WooHoo! Typically, these are experiences, interactions, activities, and ways of being in the world that make us feel energized, uplifted, alive, and present. Perhaps these are activities that feel more like play than work. Maybe they are interactions that are particularly fulfilling, or through which you feel like your involvement really matters.

There are no right or wrong answers here, just those answers that are true for you. Be wary of any thoughts that may creep in about what you "should" list, or what your family or co-workers might expect your answers to be. Let's silence those voices in your head and simply listen for that song your soul sings.

Now that you've spent some time listing experiences that make you smile, can you identify any commonalities? If you had to categorize these things into three or four big buckets, what would they be? For example, my big buckets include nature/travel adventures with my family, empowering and uplifting others, spiritual exploration, and writing/teaching. Make a note of your three or four big buckets. This will come in handy later in the book.

In following Howard Thurman's advice and discovering what makes you come alive, you gain great insight on how you can best be of service to the world. Too many people sleepwalk through life, denying themselves, and the rest of us, the benefit of their gifts, talents, and passions.

You can fall into a trap of not realizing the value of what lights you up. Maybe you think your own soul's song is common, nothing special, true for everyone. But that's simply not the case.

One of the most beautiful aspects of creation is the amazing diversity within and all around us: diversity in how we think, feel, perceive the world; diversity in what makes us tick; and, therefore, diversity in how we can serve and be served by others. However, the closer we are to something, the less appreciative of it we can be, especially when it is something as personal as our own strengths, talents, and passions.

What are your strengths? What are you ridiculously good at?

I'm serious!

Write a list of all the things you believe you are great at. This is not a comparison exercise. It is neither a time for humbleness nor self-doubt.

What do you do incredibly well? What have you done that has generated compliments or atta-girls from others? Not that recognition from others is necessary, but sometimes we may need to use them as a clue to what our strengths might be.

These strengths or talents might take the shape of an activity or a skill. Or, they could be your way of being in the world. Are you calm, peaceful, a get-it-done gal, a big idea person? The way you approach life and the world may be where you find your Inner Spark. Be creative and open-minded about what constitutes a strength.

This may be super uncomfortable for you. That's okay.

Turn off the inner critic in your mind, and let the answers flow.

Now, how does that feel? Did anything surprise you?

If you were to capture your strengths and talents and sort them into a few major categories, what would they be?

"What does all of this have to do with service?" you may ask.

When you appreciate what makes your soul sing and combine it with your strengths, you begin to understand how you can best serve the world in a way that makes a difference for others and regenerates you too.

I love to use my voice. For most people, this might mean singing. I do love to sing, typically loud and proud in the car or in the shower, preferably with enough background noise to not terrorize my family or dogs. I have also been known to lead groups in singing a rousing rendition of I'm a Little Teapot to make the point about Soulful Service. I enjoy singing, but oh, Lord, I'm terrible at it. It is definitely not a natural strength of mine. As a result, singing is not likely my unique path to service in the world. And that's completely okay. Plenty of amazing singers are out there, like my dear friend Kristen, who uses her voice and original music to lift and even heal the world. That's her gift, that's what brings her joy, and that's how she can most authentically serve others.

But I do love to speak…and I'm pretty good at it. Using my voice through speaking, teaching, leading workshops, creating videos, and even writing, is a good combination of something that lights me up (using my voice) and a strength (communicating a message).

And I love empowering and guiding others in the quest to identify what brings them joy, how they can most effectively contribute, and how they might bring this together in a balanced, energized way in their lives.

I feel most fulfilled when coupling these two elements to empower Difference Makers. That's my Inner Spark. What's yours?

Consciously connecting what lights us up with what plays to our strengths is one way to shift from exhausted to energized in our service. We can then give from our best selves in a way that regenerates rather than depletes our energy. This empowers our Soulful Service to be both more meaningful and more sustainable.

SOULFUL SERVICE CONSIDERATIONS:

What makes your soul sing?

What are your strengths or talents?

How do you currently bring your Inner Gift into your service? If you don't, why not?

How could you integrate that which makes your soul sing and your strengths in a way that makes your service even more powerful for others and fulfilling for you?

Chapter 6

Soulful Strategies for Making "Real" Real

It started with an unprovoked breakdown, an ugly cry, sob-fest in a Metro parking lot after my evening commute from D.C. back to Arlington, VA.

I thought I was doing all the right things. College. Grad School. Grades. Valedictorian. Meaningful job. Promotions. Self-sufficiency. Reasonably decent social life.

But I felt empty and joyless, which was weird, because I'm generally an optimistic, happy-go-lucky person.

"What's the problem?" my significant other at the time asked. He was a fixer, and if he knew the problem, he couldn't help but offer his version of the solution.

"I don't know."

Honest answer. It didn't make any sense to me why I felt the way I did. I had nothing to complain about. Life was good by external standards.

I had checked the right boxes. Built a nice resume. Opened doors of opportunity. Why couldn't that be enough? I truly didn't understand. Succeeding in all the "shoulds" left me empty. I knew something was missing. I simply had no idea what it was.

My soul was not singing.

Back then, my logical, smart girl brain didn't even register that soul singing was a thing.

It took me a couple more years before I began working with a fantastic coach. During one of our early discussions, Mary asked me about my values. Values? It sounded rather churchy to me. I didn't grok what values had to do with my continued state of blah.

Rather than argue, I trusted her and decided to view this exploration like the treasure hunt it was. Values. Hmm.... Interesting.

She encouraged me to quickly jot down words that were meaningful to me, concepts that I respected or admired, ways or states of being that were worth striving toward. A word nerd at heart, the invitation to play with words in this way felt more like a mysterious dance than some weird, coach-y exercise.

She asked for six words. Always the over-achiever, I came up with 34. She led me through a forced-choice process to narrow down the list and finally arrive at an identified set of values that were personally meaningful, inspiring, and empowering.

Then she asked how my current life reflected those values.

Well, crap.

There was my answer to the "what's the matter" question. I was busy doing things that didn't matter to my values. And *that was exactly the problem.*

The truth is, extensive studying and long hours at work were not reflected in my values. The work I was doing, though meaningful and for an important cause, didn't fit the bill. For me, I needed more than work for an important cause, I needed to feel like I was empowering people, making a real and direct difference in the lives of others. Sitting in a headquarters office in D.C. with limited contact with those who might ultimately benefit directly from the work we were doing was perfect to some, but it didn't light my fire.

In his book *What Matters Most,* Hyrum Smith explains it this way:

"Perhaps the most excruciating kind of pain comes from the gap—in some instances a wide chasm—between what we really value and what we are doing. This occurs when we realize that we are not living up to our potential, or, even worse, that what we are doing doesn't match or is completely in opposition to what we really value, to what matters most to us."

It took the terror attacks of 9/11, having a baby, and leaving a prestigious job on Capitol Hill before I finally started to make choices based on my self-identified set of values. That's the circuitous route, my friend. The scenic path. My hope for you is that you are already on the express train to fulfillment, or at least that once we work to find the right platform, you will choose a more intentional path.

Explore Your Values

When you can connect your values with your difference-making and your life building, magic happens. Your service becomes more soulful, and so does your life.

Much like Mary helped me identify my values all those years ago, we are now going to explore your personal values. These are not necessarily your parents' values or pulpit values, but those standards, principals, and qualities that are personally meaningful to you. As long as the answers reflect your truth, they are right. That's what Real looks and feels like. Outside opinions don't count. Your insight is all that matters here.

The following is a list of words meant to serve as a catalyst for helping you identify your values. This list is only intended to get your own creative juices flowing. The world of values is far greater than this, so dig in, try on some of these words, and feel into which concepts are the right fit for you.

WARNING: Don't for a minute think about choosing values because you think you "should." This isn't about satisfying other people or the needs of the ego. This is about identifying those values that, when you align your priorities and actions with them, might actually make your soul sing. Don't worry what others would think if they read your list. This isn't about them. This is about the way you would ideally like to be—how you want to show up in the world.

IDEAS FOR VALUES WORDS

Accomplishment	Excellence	Knowledge	Respect
Achievement	Expression	Leadership	Responsible
Adventure	Fairness	Love	Safety
Authenticity	Family	Loyalty	Self-Awareness
Community	Freedom	Mastery	Sensuality
Compassion	Generosity	Optimism	Service
Constancy	Gratitude	Order	Spirituality
Contentment	Growth	Originality	Stability
Contribution	Happiness	Peace	Strength
Cooperation	Health	Personal Growth	Success
Courage	Honesty	Playfulness	Trust
Creativity	Honor	Positivity	Understanding
Dignity	Imagination	Power	Vision
Diversity	Independence	Recognition	Vitality
Dependability	Integrity	Relationships	Wealth
Empathy	Joy	Relaxation	Wisdom
Equality	Kindness	Renewal	Zeal

Values: What's Real for You

Working in either your own journal or the *Real. Big. Love. Workbook,* brainstorm and choose up to eight values for yourself. These are words/ideas that reflect what is important to you, qualities that you would like to have guide your life and decisions, ways in which you would like to show up in the world.

If you are a Word Nerd overachiever like me and come up with a long list, rank the values or score them to see which ones rise to the top as the most important to you.

If this still feels incomplete, consider whether a couple of the values might fit under another term that can encompass multiple meanings. For example, in my list of values, I chose the umbrella term "vitality" to cover health, energy, and overall mental, physical, and emotional well-being. An umbrella value might be appropriate for you too.

How do these words feel? Do they seem to capture your essence? If I saw your values, would I feel like I know you a bit better, like I know what makes you tick?

I created my value list while living and working in the D.C. area and before becoming a mom. I assumed that having a baby and moving back to Oklahoma might change the values that were important to me. Interestingly, rather than the values changing, their importance to me actually grew.

When we are on track with our fundamental values, big shifts can reinforce them rather than make them waiver.

This was never more apparent than when I said "Yes!" to being an adult chaperone on a 10-day backpacking trip in the Rocky Mountains with kids who, due to the circumstances of their lives, needed positive adult role models and a healthy dose of positive direction.

I visited the local council on youth services to talk with the leadership about a grant-writing project. When Cindy, now the executive director, looked at me and said, "You need to go with us," I had no idea what she was talking about. She explained the program and that the group is always in need of women to serve as chaperones on the co-ed wilderness trips. Before my brain could argue, an enthusiastic "Yes!" came straight from my heart and out my mouth.

Here's the deal. At the time, I was pushing 40, at least 60 pounds overweight, not incredibly active, and had never been on a multi-day, dig-a-hole-for-a-bathroom kind of backpacking trip. Driving home, my mind came up with 10,000 reasons why this was a bad idea, but my soul was singing. Honestly, I was a bit confused. Why did this feel so right?

It wasn't until after the trip that it dawned on me. This opportunity was in complete alignment with every single one of my values. Being of service through a challenging wilderness adventure allowed me to feel more like me.

When an opportunity speaks directly to your fundamental values, saying yes feels natural, and the reward is meaningful.

This is still one of my very favorite, most memorable experiences. I'm so glad that in the split second before I said yes, my heart overpowered my brain to allow me to live into what mattered most for me.

I've also found that when making decisions between multiple possible options, if I return to my list of values and determine how each would be served through a decision, the choice becomes much clearer.

Recognizing and honoring your personal values can bring clarity and purpose to your choices and help you feel more satisfied with both the journey and the destination.

Starring Roles

In addition to values, we'll also consider the roles you play in your life. Nope, I'm not referring to the on-stage-with-a-dramatic-flair variety, but the more Real, sometimes mundane, but always important roles that you play on a daily or at least regular basis. These roles might be personal, professional, service-oriented, passion-driven, or any other combination. Some may feel exciting and energizing, others may feel like a drag on your energy. This exploration is simply about taking inventory of where you share your energy now.

In the *Real. Big. Love. Workbook* or in your journal, brainstorm all the roles you play in your life. Volunteer, employee, parent, spouse, daughter, musician, writer, runner, outdoor enthusiast, Mahjong champion, artist, community advocate, karaoke superstar, etc. You get the picture. Simply list all the different hats you wear in your life.

Many of my clients find that once they really begin listing the roles they play, the list grows long very quickly.

How does your list feel? Does it seem complete? Are you surprised? When you look at the list, does it feel motivating or exhausting?

Recently I asked Lynne to brainstorm aloud all the roles she plays in her life. She came up with 16 before she even had to start thinking too hard. She was surprised to recognize all the places her time, attention, and energy go, and all the different directions in which she feels pulled. "No wonder I'm exhausted all the time," she said.

When Hillary and I talked about the list of roles she created, she admitted she felt a bit "meh" looking at it. As we talked about why that was, it quickly became apparent that her list of roles did not include the thing that made her soul sing—being a musician. She was so focused on her roles doing for others that she forgot to include the role that fed her passion and refueled her energy. Once we added musician to the list, she felt energized and excited about stepping more into the role that clearly lights her up from the inside.

If you came up with more than eight roles, consider combining some of the roles in a broader category. For example, on my original list I listed Mom, Wife, and Daughter/Sister as separate categories. Later I condensed them into one role category called "Family Member." Each relationship is different and requires different attention and energy, so for you, listing them separately might make more sense.

My "Difference Maker" category includes a number of different volunteer and teaching roles, including adjunct teaching, serving as a board member, volunteering, leading workshops, etc.

I divide my business-related roles. One deals with content creation and providing service, the other deals with actually managing the details of the business, like accounting and marketing. These are different enough for me that I need to keep them distinct in order to make progress on either or both.

As long as the role categories make sense to you, that's all that matters. Make sure you have at least one category to account for your Difference Maker role. This category can represent any way that you volunteer, support, or work to uplift others, a cause, an organization, etc. These might be official roles within organizations, a non-official role with a community or religious organization, or formal or informal efforts to lift up, clean up, or offer a hand up to others or a cause. As a Difference Maker, you need to make sure that your Difference Maker role is accounted for.

Now, in your list of roles, did you include one that is specifically designed to nurture, care for, and look out for you? If you did, hallelujah, you are ahead of the curve. If not, you are completely normal and likely someone who consistently puts the needs of others before your own. This falls squarely in the selfless service category, and while noble, can be quite hard to sustain.

To step into Soulful Service, we need to dedicate at least one of our roles to looking out for and tending to our own well-being.

The same client who started with 16 original roles did not include a single one dedicated to looking out for her. It was no surprise that she found it difficult to prioritize time for her health, which was her most pressing immediate concern. Once I pointed this out, she immediately recognized that adding a role as her own Health Champion could help her keep her own health and well-being on the front instead of the back burner.

We can offer even better service to the world, make a bigger difference, and impact more lives when we invest in our own energy, vitality, and well-being.

"Yeah, but ... I don't have the time, I don't have the money, others need me more," and on and on....

I know. I've heard all the excuses. Hell, I've given all the excuses. But deep down, we both know that someone needs to look out for you too. And you are not likely to ask for that kind of support or assistance from others. It's up to you, friend.

In the interviews, client work, and conversations that helped guide the creation of this work, those who felt the most energy and who felt the least stress were those who recognized that their well-being was their responsibility and that others benefitted when they made a point to tend to it.

So please consider adding "Self-Advocate" or "Self-Champion" or "Self-Coach" or something similar to your roles list to ensure that you make yourself a priority. Don't let this feel selfish. Remember that when you focus a role to keep your teapot full and your energy up, others benefit even more from your Soulful Service.

Now, I'd like you to consider some roles to give up. Of course, these roles were not on your list, but if they sound familiar, it's time to let them go. People Pleaser, Yes Person, Doormat, Unappreciated Chauffeur, Doomsday Scenarioist, Martyr, Victim, Uninspired or Dispassionate Servant.

The roles to give up are those that drown out the song of your soul, are inconsistent with your values, make you feel like crap, make you stay small, feel suffocating, or in any other manner dim your light.

The context and situation you currently find yourself in can also significantly shape how you view your role. For too many years, the role of "wife" felt like a wet blanket on my joy. Today, "wife" feels like an uplifted, supported, and encouraging role. My context for the role changed when I got divorced and eventually remarried, and so did my enjoyment of it.

Unfortunately, my husband recently had an opposite experience. After working for the same company for nearly 20 years, the last 11 in a supervisory role, he was recruited by another company to perform a similar function. The former company motivated employees through incentives, positive communication, common training, camaraderie, and encouragement. He loved helping employees come up with positive solutions to challenges and encouraging them to do their best. This approach is in alignment with his core values.

In stark contrast, the second company motivated by fear and

perpetual threat of employees losing their jobs. Interestingly enough, this fear-based approach was even spelled out in the Supervisors' Handbook, which he didn't have the luxury to read until after he was hired.

This shift of context caused my husband to be miserable in his job. It was out of alignment with his own value of being a positive influence on the lives of others. Although the mechanics and basic job descriptions were the same, the role felt completely different. The last job was completely draining on his energy, emotions, and overall well-being.

When it comes to roles, context matters.

Part of your opportunity in your role as "Self-Advocate" is to determine the context and conditions that most help you shine and feel buoyant in your roles, and to make shifts as needed.

If we are being Real, then we need to be Real in all our roles. Not just the roles where it's easy. Not just the roles where people love you no matter what. All our roles. When we feel the need to muzzle ourselves, to hide our true nature, or to twist and contort ourselves to meet the expectations of others, we lose energy and feel out of integrity with ourselves.

Clarity about your values can help you make choices that light you up from the inside. When you are clear about the roles in which you serve, you can make decisions that support enjoyment in those roles. When you connect your values and your roles with your strengths and what makes your soul sing, you discover your Real treasures.

Role Assessment

1. Role Satisfaction

Now that you've identified each role, determine how satisfied you are with your experience of each role. How well do you feel like you are doing in this particular area of your life? In your journal or the workbook, write each of your eight roles on a separate line. Then, rate your level of satisfaction for each role on a scale of 1–10, with one being "I'm miserable in this role" and ten being "WooHoo! This role lights me up!"

It's unrealistic to think that you might be a 10 right now in each role. Don't set that expectation for yourself and think that anything less means failure. The purpose of this exercise is to become aware of how well you believe you are showing up in each role. Don't expect perfection. Don't beat yourself up. And this isn't about how other people perceive you in this role. This is about how you perceive you. For right now, your opinion is the only one that counts.

2. **Role Intention**

    Next, rate the level of intention with which you approach each role. In some roles we may be more proactive, setting goals for ourselves or envisioning an outcome to strive toward. In other roles we may be more reactive, dealing with stuff as it gets thrown our way.

    Really think about how consciously you choose your actions, the intentional energy you put into each role. Are you acting on purpose toward some bigger goal, or in response to immediate needs and external stimuli? Again, this is not a place for judgment about the answers, simply an opportunity for honest awareness and assessment.

3. **Role Alignment with Values**

    How are your values reflected in each of your roles? Too often, we may think of our values only in a specific situation or when making a specific decision. If we integrate our values throughout how we live into each of our roles, how we act through these roles, and how we serve in each role, then we amplify our opportunity for authentically meaningful impact.

Give yourself a score from 1–10 for how well each of your values is reflected in each role. The easiest way to do this is to create a grid that lists your roles vertically along the left side and your values horizontally across the top. Where each intersect, write a number.

Be kind. Don't overthink this. Be honest. This assessment is simply a snapshot of this current moment in time.

How well are your values reflected in the roles you play? Now, look back at your level of satisfaction with each role. Do you notice anything?

When clients find that they have low scores on Role Satisfaction, they also tend to notice lower scores in how much their values are reflected in that role.

Identifying values and roles is more than an interesting concept. It can be an effective compass to help keep you on track, so that both your service and your life are living, breathing reflections of that which is most important to you. When you couple your values with your strengths and passions, and intentionally bring that secret sauce into the way you show up in each of your roles, the world, your relationships, and your life will benefit.

When your role as a Difference Maker and your values align, and when you are intentional about your contribution, you begin to hit Soulful Service gold.

SOULFUL SERVICE CONSIDERATIONS:

How are your values reflected in the ways you serve?

How intentional are you in your Difference Maker role?

Do you view prioritizing your own self-care as
an important element in any of your roles?

How might you be able to better reflect
your values in each role?

> *You are braver than you believe,*
> *and stronger tha you seem,*
> *and smarter than you think.*
>
> *~ Christopher Robin to Winnie the Pooh*

Part 2: BIG

PLAYING BIG FOR SOULFUL SERVICE:

- Soulful Service invites you to move beyond your comfort zone to make an even more profound difference.

- Soulful Service focuses not on grandiosity, but on meaningfulness to drive a Big contribution.

- Soulful Service asks that you invest your Bigness—your full, whole self—into your difference-making.

- Soulful Service values consistency of effort, recognizing that even small actions done with great consistency can yield Big results.

Chapter 7

Playing Big Rather than Settling for Small

My dear mom is not a fan of public speaking. Like, not at all. She is traumatized by the queasy, nervous, might-pass-out kind of fear that she normally reserves solely for the snakes that randomly show up in her garage.

That said, when given the opportunity to talk about the importance of early breast cancer detection, she gladly steps up to the microphone. Mom has dedicated her entire career to the health care field in radiology, and, in these years inching toward retirement, has focused exclusively on performing mammograms. She connects with women (and men) every day who hope for a clean scan, or who may be returning if something shows up.

As a breast cancer survivor, Mom is particularly aware of the importance of early detection to address the cancer before it grows and spreads. She is committed to increasing awareness about the importance of regular self-breast exams and mammograms in order to help save lives. In this case, passion for her cause outweighs the discomfort of public speaking. She chooses to act Big and not stay small, because the lives of others could hang in the balance.

Big looks different for every single person. For Mom, it's public speaking. For me, it's writing and publishing this book, the first time I taught college classes inside a men's prison, or choosing to re-launch my business because I believe it's how I can best serve in a Bigger way.

Big is anything that puts us outside our comfort zone in order to make a difference for ourselves or others.

Playing small does no favors for those we seek to serve.

This one concept was a life-changing kick in the pants for me. Our fear, our worries, and our concerns get in the way of us being of service to those who could benefit from our unique brand of help. In keeping our gifts to ourselves, we are selfishly denying their benefit in the world.

If we want to be Difference Makers, then we have to step up, speak up, and lift up our cause. Being a Difference Maker committed to Soulful Service requires that we step out of our comfort zone.

Maybe you already put your all into your cause and play big for others. Or you might be completely exhausted and even a bit shell-shocked by the demands and needs that making a difference requires. You don't have another ounce of energy or courage to spare. You may have even grown reluctantly and unconsciously apathetic from feeling like you're beating your head against a wall without obvious support or progress for too long.

If your service or your life has taken on more of a "HoHum" rather than "WooHoo" quality, something is likely holding you back. Whether it feels like obstacles or shackles or quicksand, rather than give up or give in, let's identify the challenge and the comfort-zone-busting solution.

This is in no way an indictment on your effort or a reason to feel bad or guilty regarding your service. Just the opposite. If there's even a tinge of guilt, that's simply because you deeply care about how you serve. You genuinely want to make a meaningful difference for others.

Stuff gets in the way. It's normal. Sometimes, most of the time, it's your own stuff.

We believe in changing the world. We often see the change needed as entirely external. However, it might be that the first and biggest difference you can make for your cause is how you approach your service. It's an inside job. It's where Gandhi tried to lead us with the encouragement to "be the change you wish to see in the world."

Service-Wrecking F-Bombs

I've noticed a few four-letter F-bombs that can wreak havoc on our service and in our lives. These F-bombs tend to keep us playing small. They seek to keep us firmly in our comfort zone. They seek to keep us safe. Despite the potentially noble façade, there's nothing innocuous about these little buggers and the ways we allow them far too much power and control over our lives.

Fear. Fail. Fine.

Little words that can create big roadblocks.

It was a simple walk to the corner Starbucks. A colleague and I were making a quick coffee run to refuel for an afternoon of deadlines. The conversation got deep, and he finally said, "You know, you could do amazing things if you would just get out of your own way."

Ouch.

It hadn't dawned on me before how much time I spent stymying my own progress, talking myself out of opportunities, playing small instead of stepping into Big.

It didn't make any sense. When I fully engaged, my track record was strong, so why did I allow self-created fear to keep me from making a bigger difference? I now realize that I was allowing Fear, Fail, and Fine to steal the best of me.

The truth is that most of us, in some way or another, get in our own way. It's normal. What's less common is realizing when we do it. That's where a bit of self-awareness or blunt friends can come in handy. Either can help us identify the four-letter F-bombs that risk effing up our service and our lives.

Fear

Fear is a beast. It can stop us in our tracks, keep us playing small, and tempt us to give up before we even begin. Fear can make us choose not to serve, or not to live in a bigger way, because Big is uncomfortable or new. Fear keeps us firmly in our comfort zone, casting shadow on our Light and diminishing our impact.

What is fear, really? Some have described fear as False Evidence Appearing Real. Our brains are tricky little suckers and are on a constant mission to keep us safe, comfortable, and out of harm's way. Our brains might see a challenge, see someone who looks differently, see a big need, and then try to come up with all the reasons we should run the other way.

However, the opportunity to make our biggest difference is typically on the other side of our comfort zone. If we let fear run the show, we'd never be in the difference-making game. It's often messy and hard, and we are not guaranteed to win.

I felt fear the day I was told I would be leading a college program that offered associates degrees on-site at two nearby state correctional centers. I had never been to a prison. I had no idea what to expect. I'd seen movies and heard unpleasant stories from relatives and friends who worked in maximum security facilities. People even asked who I had pissed off to get this assignment.

While I didn't completely chicken out and say, "No way," I was admittedly super apprehensive the first day I taught at the men's prison. Twenty-five convicted male felons, me, a classroom with no cameras, no nearby guard. Just a blackboard, some chalk, and an American Federal Government textbook.

What could possibly go wrong?

Nothing went wrong. Students were eager to learn. I was eager to teach. We all learned something new about the subject and about ourselves. I continue to teach college classes at the prisons today.

My initial fear was rooted in placing more emphasis on the label "convicted felon" than on the label "student," or better yet, "human being." But now that I've had the opportunity to teach in a number of settings, teaching inside the prisons is my favorite. When people are committed to their own progress and building a real second chance for their future, good things take place.

I'm thankful I didn't allow my initial fear to prevent me from having this experience. Sure, I take precautions to stay safe and don't drop my guard. But I genuinely appreciate the chance to contribute to other human beings creating more positive opportunities for their life.

Are there areas in which you let fear stand in the way of your service? Remember, fear is normal; it is our brain's way of trying to keep us safe. When fear shows up, know that you are not alone. And, sometimes the fear is incredibly justified.

For each of us, our opportunity is to really look at the fear and decide if it's rational, if we can take steps to lessen it, or if we need to rely more on the antidote to Fear, which I believe is Faith.

Even when we cannot be completely certain of an outcome, having faith in ourselves, in the Divine, in the Universe, whatever you place faith in, can be a powerful tool for feeling the fear and serving anyway.

Or, in the insightful wisdom of Jen Sincero, author of *You Are a Badass*, "Faith is the audacity to believe in the not-yet-seen," and "Faith is your best buddy when you're scared shitless."

Fail

When I left my job as a US Senate Communication Director to raise my daughter and eventually start a consulting practice, I decided I also wanted to volunteer to help uplift others in some way. After a lot of thought, including weighing where I felt the time investment would yield the biggest return for someone else, I decided to volunteer as a literacy tutor and help adults gain the gift of words.

I was paired with my first student. We were to meet for the first time at a public library in a suburb of Washington, D.C. Gia looked like a tough one. She was wearing a huge, puffy coat, a knit cap pulled down to her eyes, heavy work boots, and what appeared to be a reluctant attitude. If she was trying to intimidate me, it was working. Who did I think I was to be able to teach another adult how to read?

But I knew this first interaction would make or break our ability to successfully work together. There was no way I was going to let uncertainty stand in the way.

If I was at all concerned, I could only imagine that her fears were ten times higher. Gia was a single mom of three in her forties, worked full time, and didn't know the alphabet, much less how to read or write. She had tried to learn to read before. She was no dummy, but none of her previous efforts had worked out. She had reservations about this time, too, and didn't want to feel like a failure again.

My goal in this first meeting was to help her feel at ease and for her to want to meet again. At this point, I knew that building a relationship was more important than learning letters. If we could form a bond, then maybe together, we could both get over our fear of failing.

A year and a half later, not only could she recite the alphabet, she could read books—and even won an essay contest through the local literacy council. I was incredibly proud of her progress and her willingness to keep trying even when it was hard.

In celebration, I invited Gia to join me at a Barbara Bush Foundation literacy fundraising event in Richmond, VA. When I picked her up to ride together, I was blown away by how much she had changed since our first meeting. Sure, her appearance was different—heels and hose, professional dress, beautiful hair, makeup and nails—but what struck me most was her confidence. That night, Gia beamed from the inside out. She persisted and accomplished what she thought might be impossible. She was proud of herself, and it was beautiful.

When we allow, "What if I fail?" to get in the way, we steal our own success.

In the beginning, Gia got more words wrong than she got right. But she kept trying.

We will fail. The trick is to be willing to persist.

For her, learning to read was like eating an elephant: the only way to do it was one bite, one word, one sentence at a time. She was never going to be able to snap her fingers and magically know how to read. But one word to the next, one sentence to the next, one paragraph and one page to the next, her little successes grew into a huge life-changing win for her.

There is a Japanese proverb that is my favorite definition of success: Fall down seven times; stand up eight. Gia kept standing up.

When we let the possibility of failing keep us out of the game, we never get to flex our grit muscles.

A friend recently explained that failure is a state of mind. "For me, failure is not an option. How you look at it determines whether it's a failure. Things may not have worked out the way I initially thought, but it's still not a failure."

We live. We learn. We grow. We move on.

In an effort to prevent failure, we may cling to the idea of doing something perfectly.

Nice try.

What if we simply accept that "perfect" in an illusion that keeps us stuck? The need for "perfect" leads to procrastination, maybe even to giving up before we ever really get going. We won't be perfect when we start, regardless of how much natural talent, brains, support, or insight we have. We will mess up. It is okay.

The antidote to Fail is Fortitude.

We persist. We keep going. We turn the idea of failure on its head so that we experience a learning opportunity every time we don't quite succeed. Genuinely, the only way to truly fail is to never try, or to quit before we learn something useful.

Our causes, our people, our communities, our world, need us to stay committed and keep trying. Fortitude makes that possible in the face of unavoidable struggle.

Fine

Fine. Ugh. This is one of my least favorite words.

"How are you doing?"

"Oh, you know, I'm fine."

I call bullshit on Fine.

Fine is typically a thinly-veiled disguise for "I've lost my spark," or "Things in my life kind of suck, but I can't let you know that," or "I'm so overwhelmed, but I'm putting on a good show."

Fine can also signify frustration or even apathy.

Fine is often an unconscious plea for someone to dig deeper and draw out the Real truth. As people who serve and who juggle much in doing so, we don't want to show any cracks. We don't want to worry folks. We don't want to need to ask for help. Instead, we resort to Fine and the hope that someday we won't feel like we are drowning in our responsibilities.

Where in your life or service are you settling for "fine?" How would your life or service be different if you lit it up, threw some passion and energy into it, lived into it with purpose? Would life be better than fine if you weren't juggling so many balls, if you did get some help, or if you felt more passion and energy?

Don't you want life to be better than fine?

The antidote to Fine is Fullness.

Fullness. Not in a busy, full schedule sense, but in a deep, nurtured, meaningful, richness of experience sense. We overcome Fine when we feel Full, we feel nurtured, and we feel like our time, energy, and love investments are meaningful.

Fullness includes recognizing and honoring those elements of your life that are meaningful to you. Maybe you have a hobby that lights you up, but you've put it on the backburner while you see to the needs of others. Maybe regular exercise gives you more energy and vitality to tackle your day and to-do list, but it's been one of those things that hasn't been getting done.

I work with Difference Makers to explore those things that bring them a sense of Fullness and then help them figure out how to prioritize them in their lives. Interestingly, instead of feeling like it's one more damn thing they need to fit into an already crowded schedule, they usually end up feeling less stressed, less exhausted, and more balanced as a result.

When you take the time to feel into what lights you up, what brings you joy, and even what wears you out, you begin to craft a framework for your life and your service that replaces the dreaded Fine with the no-longer-elusive Full.

Here's the deal with Fear, Fail, and Fine: We will experience each of them. We are human. We are not immune to these F-bombs. They are sneaky little brain twisters that are very good at persuading us to get, and sometimes stay, in our own way.

Do you really want to give them that much power? There's no need to let them become your kryptonite. When you recognize Fear, Fail, and Fine for what they are, and then remember the antidotes of Faith, Fortitude, and Fullness, you can shift these F-bombs, from being destructive forces that keep you small, to becoming the fertilizer that helps you bloom.

F-Bomb Detection Exercises

How are you in the F-bomb department? Are Fear, Fail, and Fine effing with your ability to serve or your ability to fully live your life? Let's get specific and see how they might be holding you back or preventing you from fully serving your cause or enjoying your life.

Fear: In your journal or the workbook, please list any fears that come to mind that might be getting in the way of your service or your life. These fears can be big or small. They can come with internal or external rationale or potential consequences. Don't spend too much time analyzing them right now. In working with clients, some common fears I hear are:

"What will people think?"

"I'm not good enough/don't know enough/haven't had enough school to do that."

"What if I make a fool of myself?"

"What if I lose _____?" (job, spouse, kids, dignity, respect, house, etc.)

"I might die, or be injured, or face certain doom."

"Haters... what if the haters come after me on social media?"

"Who do I think I am to _____?"

"What if I fail?"

What are yours? What current or past fears stand in your way of making a bigger difference for your cause or in your life?

This exercise can sometimes be painful or cause you to name a fear that you haven't fully explored before. In my work with clients, we search for the underlying thoughts that drive these fears and then work to turn those thoughts on their head. Often, it's a perspective shift, or a subtle new way of looking at things that can make a significant difference in either loosening the grip of the fear or finding the faith and courage to feel the fear and take action anyway.

Now, let's look at fear from one other perspective. When it comes to your cause or your life, what do you fear *not* happening? Or, what do you fear will happen if you don't act Big to do something about it? Again, write these thoughts in your journal or workbook.

Which of these two lists of fears concerns you more—the list of fears or the list of consequences when fear runs the show?

Interestingly, fear can either cause paralysis, or it can become an extraordinary motivator to finally move forward in a big way. When fear is a motivator, it is because we keep our eye on the difference we want to make, our big why, and allow that to be more powerful at creating momentum than fear is at stopping us in our tracks.

Someone once asked me to explain my biggest fear. After a bit of consideration, I realized that, at that time, my biggest fear was to never know the true extent of my potential. Staying small is a sure-fire way to ensure that *my* biggest fear is fully realized.

No, thank you.

We have a much better opportunity to avoid our biggest fears if we act through our biggest selves, our full selves.

Fail: Many of us see success and failure as black and white, win and loss. Often, our notion of failure is based on external expectations and circumstances. Again, a perspective shift can turn a failure into a learning opportunity. Thinking only of the present and toward the future, do you see any areas in your life or your service where you either feel you are currently failing, or fear that you will fail? Write them in your journal or workbook.

When I'm working with clients, it's at this point that we assess how real their concerns about failure are, determine if those concerns warrant action or a perspective shift, and plan out ways to either prevent failure from happening or to repair the damage if it does and learn from it. Realistic, workable options take the disempowering poison out of the idea of failure.

We also analyze the cost of inaction. What is lost if fear of failure wins? Typically, that answer becomes motivation enough to overpower both Fear and Fail with a healthy dose of inspired action.

Fine: How often do you claim "Fine" when someone asks about your health, day, service, or life? Is that response a big Band-Aid over something not-so-fine? If you were being really honest, what are those parts of your life or service that you claim are fine, but really aren't? In what areas does Fine get in the way of taking action and making meaningful progress? Write out your answers.

Fear, Fail, and Fine are all heads on the same dragon. Faith, Fortitude, and Fullness are all ways to redirect the dragon and move beyond it. You may never completely slay the dragon, and that's okay. But you don't have to let it keep you small or undermine the difference you can make for your cause and in your life.

SOULFUL SERVICE CONSIDERATIONS:

How do you apply Faith in your service or life? How could you?

How's your Fortitude factor? Where have you learned from supposed failure and kept moving forward? What current challenges can you apply that approach to?

In what areas of your life do you currently feel less than Full? How does that affect your service?

In what areas of your life do you feel Full? How does that influence your service? How can you bring more Fullness to the areas that feel flat?

CHAPTER 8

Put Your Whole Self in— Playing Hokey-Pokey with Service and Life

The whole concept of Big used to really turn me off. I equated Big with the size of my ass, big egos, being "too big for my britches," and a host of other unsavory things.

Then I began to see big through a different lens. As my daughter grew and yearned to be "big," I saw that as her desire to step into her own unfolding potential.

Big became a synonym for brave, having the courage to step outside that comfort zone.

Big became a touchstone for consistency—even small actions, done consistently, can lead to Big results.

Big also became meaningful, in the sense that even if you don't save the entire world through your service, you can make a Big (meaningful) contribution for others.

Big came to mean whole, full.

Playing Big, I came to see as the flip side of staying small.

If you can bring your whole, full self with courage and consistency to your cause, then you increase your odds of making a meaningful difference. That is Big. And you boost your chances of being satisfied with your investment in the outcome. You actually engage in Soulful Service.

Now, after rethinking Big, I see it as a term filled with beauty and potential, not one filled with annoyance and ego.

Big service. Big impact. Big love. Big doesn't have to denote grandiose or outrageous. It's not about size. It's about commitment, courage, and how much of yourself you offer to the outcome.

We're talking about a willingness to play Big with your investment of yourself in your cause and your life here. Are you willing to put your whole self in to make a difference? Or, will you be playing hokey-pokey with those things that mean the most to you?

Some of us are great at putting part of ourselves in. Maybe we invest our mind, or our money, or our time. We put our time in, we take our time out, we put our time in, and we shake it all about....

How's that working?

If you serve from your fullness, rather than in dribs and drabs, into the causes you care about, Real, Big, Love-driven outcomes can happen.

Am I asking you to sacrifice your well-being and your energy to a cause? Of course not. That's not sustainable. Now that you've discovered your unique gift of service, your WooHoo contribution, we want to make sure you're not half-assing how you show up with it. Your Inner Gift is not present in one segregated part of you, it expresses itself throughout all of you—not just your mind or your voice or your pocketbook, but it shows up in its fullness when you show up in your fullness.

Believe it or not, showing up fully is a lot less exhausting than trying to hide, muzzle, deny, or reject integral pieces of yourself.

I am asking you to consider how you invest your mind, your heart, your body, your spirit, your energy, your voice, your resources, and your connection in making a difference.

Whew. That may feel like a lot. The point here is not to be overwhelming, but to consider how you contribute from all those amazing places that are uniquely you.

When I worked with Kris, she and I got to the root of why her accounting position with the nonprofit she loved didn't light her up. It wasn't the organization or the cause or the people. It was the actual position. She followed in her mom's footsteps when she chose accounting, knowing that it was a secure career path with plenty of jobs.

Kris was great at engaging her brain in the mental activity of managing the finances. But she was a people person at heart. She longed to interact with people more than with numbers. As we talked through her dissatisfaction at work, we realized she was pigeon-holed in this one position, and that prevented her from serving with the fullness of her gifts.

Once she talked with the executive director, they were able to draw upon her as an asset to the organization and re-envision her position so that she was able to interact more with the community and even take the lead in planning major events.

This shift brought new energy to Kris. Not only did she enjoy her job more, but she soon also began taking better care of herself.

Positive changes in one area can have a ripple effect on others.

Some causes may only be interested in one aspect of your potential contribution. Maybe they want your money or your time or your influence. Since you are reading this book, though, I'm betting that you are driven to make a bigger, deeper difference.

Transformational Difference Makers are those who apply more than their resources to the art of service. They also look for ways to invest their body, mind, heart, and spirit, as well as their voice, energy, and community, in their advocacy. At this level, service is not transactional, but it is based on a depth and connection that makes real, lasting, meaningful change more possible.

True transformation is the goal of Soulful Service.

Transformational difference-making doesn't only happen in organizations or for causes. You can inspire transformational differences in your family, in your home, and in your own life.

When I tell my daughter, "I love you with my whole heart," she used to argue and say, "No, you love Grammy too, so you can't love me with all your heart." My opportunity was to help her realize that there's no part of my heart with which I don't love her. I'm holding nothing back. I can love multiple people (and in my case, puppies) with all my heart. She seemed to understand that explanation.

The same is true with service. If we engage with our resources, but hold back our hearts, our voice, or our Inner Spark, then we are denying an important part of our whole self to our service. If we are passionate about making a difference, why would we hold back the vital parts of ourselves that can help us make our most important contribution?

We rarely make meaningful connections with our brains or our pocketbooks alone.

To offer our whole, Big self to our cause, we need to be willing to own that our ideas, thoughts, experiences, feelings, insights, and inspirations are worthy and needed for change. If we doubt the value of our contribution, we may never end up contributing it.

When we hold back our gifts and wisdom, we deny both sides of the equation—we deny ourselves the chance to share, and we deny our cause the gift of our insight. No one wins in that scenario.

When we stay cooped up in our head, the prominent domain of the three F-Bombs, we deny the gift of our full self.

Yes, you have a beautiful, wonderful brain. It is capable of deep insights, meaningful planning, and so much more. But the mind can also be a tyrant. The Bully Brain can plant seeds of doubt that undermine your potential and deny your full service and joy.

Remember, most fear is the brain's way of trying to keep you safe. Staying small seems safer than feeling uncomfortable. Stretching your limits, putting your whole self in, feels vulnerable and scary. Our brains, when stuck in fear mode, want to keep us firmly in the safety box. If we dare step into the world of Big, the Bully Brain may berate us or make us question who we think we are to even consider that we can do this.

Do you really want to give your Bully Brain that much power? When the brain runs the show, we too often deny ourselves the opportunity to serve Big, love Big, or experience Big joy.

When the brain is buttressed with the heart, the body, and the spirit, they can work as a more balanced, holistic team. It is through this wholeness that your soulful version of Big service evolves and surfaces. It is through wholeness of self that your opportunity for transformational leadership or transformational contribution grows wings.

When you step into and share your Real self and your Big self, you have the potential to reach others and promote your cause in a more meaningful way. When you show up authentically and courageously, your service becomes more inspirational and motivational and is better able to have a more lasting impact.

Your passion deserves that. The people and causes you care about need that.

In addition to looking at how you engage your mind, body, heart, and soul, I ask that you also look at your energy levels, how you use your voice, how you engage abundance and resources, and your support community. These eight spheres offer a clearer picture of where and how you are investing in your cause and your life, and where you might be holding back or even suppressing your potential impact.

Kris used her voice to ask for what she needed. Then, rather than just invest her mind and time in the accounting job, her scope grew, and she was able to offer more of herself in a way that lit her up, was more satisfying, and ultimately was more effective for the organization.

The actual practice of consistently putting your whole self in takes time, consistency, and patience. Soulful Service, Big service, may feel uncomfortable at first, but as you see and feel the difference it makes for those you serve and for yourself, you'll open the door to new levels of meaning, contribution, and personal fulfillment.

SOULFUL SERVICE CONSIDERATIONS:

From which part of yourself do you predominantly serve?

Is there a portion of yourself that you withhold from your service, either intentionally or subconsciously?

Is there a part of you that you are scared to share through your service?

How could showing up fully from all parts of yourself improve your contribution to your cause?

CHAPTER 9

Soulful Assessment to Support Big Service

To bring our whole self to our service and our life requires us to look at how we show up in eight key ways. The integration of these eight spheres can empower us to make an even bigger difference through our service and to enjoy our lives in a deeper, richer way.

This image included throughout this book is called the Seed of Life. Seven interlocking circles create the central image, with an eighth circle providing a container for the magic.

So far, all of our self-exploration exercises have involved units of eight—eight values, eight roles, and now eight areas of self-awareness and care. There's a reason for this. Eight (8), to me, is a number that represents balance, harmony, and sustainability. Like an upright infinity sign, the line is unbroken and gives a sense of continuation. Some even denote 8 as a symbol for where spirit and matter meet. That's the essence of Soulful Service—offering our Inner Gifts, our spirit, through action in the world in a balanced, sustainable manner.

In this chapter, we will briefly explore each of the Eight Spheres of Soulful Self-Care, and then we will assess the extent to which you engage in each of these areas. Finally, building on the idea that even small steps done consistently can lead to a Big impact, we'll take a look at how you attend to these eight spheres.

When I first asked Kris to complete this assessment, she rolled her eyes and huffed like a teenager. Knowing where she stood in these areas was the *last* thing she wanted to "waste" her time on. With a little persuading, she finally agreed.

By the end, she realized that it was a needed wake-up call to pull her head out of the sand and be willing to look at some of the areas in her life that she completely ignored. Rather than let her beat herself up over the low scores, we quickly identified priorities areas where she could make changes. Without the self-assessment, she may have never championed her own progress.

Hillary was a different story. After completing the self-assessment, she was pretty excited with how much she attended to most of the areas. She had a meaningful, consistent plan in place that included going to the gym, regular therapy, support from a strong tribe of encouraging women, and regularly attending church. She, too, saw areas she wanted to improve. She quickly started a blog (voice), and attended training to become a Mental Health First Aid trainer (mind) and a Master Hand Bell Conductor (community and heart). These spoke to the core of what makes her soul sing.

This self-assessment is simply a snapshot in time of how you rate yourself right now in the eight areas. There is no expectation of perfection. In fact, I'd call BS if you rated a 10 in every category. This is simply an exercise in awareness so that we can celebrate success and identify opportunities to make progress, as needed.

Sphere #1: Body   Rating (1–10) _____

Sphere #1 corresponds with your physical body. This is *not* an assessment of how happy you are with its shape or size. Instead we are looking at how much you engage the physical you in your service and in your life. Overall, do you feel fairly healthy, or are you dealing with a physical challenge? Do you move your body regularly? How are your sleep habits? How about nutrition and water consumption? Do you carry stress in your body, or are you fairly relaxed? Again, this is not a judgment exercise, but a simple observation and assessment of how your body is serving you and your service right now. Simply give Sphere #1 a rating from 1 to 10, with one being the lowest (terrible situation) to ten being the highest (plenty of physical resources to live and serve at a high level).

Sphere #2: Mind   Rating (1–10)_____

Sphere #2 refers to your mind, the mental aspects of your life. For this area, we are looking at how well your mind helps to serve your plans, purposes, and service. Do you continue to learn new things and "grow your brain"? Is the Bully Brain a perpetual and disempowering force? Do you give yourself pep talks throughout the day, especially when things get tough? Does your mind like to focus on fear and potential failure, or does it seek opportunities to grow? Overall, would you say that your thoughts help you step into a bigger version of yourself, or do your thoughts keep you small?

Sphere #3: Heart   Rating (1–10)_____

Sphere #3 explores the heart, or our feeling self. How would you rate the overall openness of your heart? Are you able/willing to acknowledge your feelings? Do you find that you are more sensitive than you would like to be, or are you a tough nut to crack in the feeling department? How would you rate your level of compassion for others, your desire to help uplift others, to recognize beauty, to grieve for loss? Are you living exclusively from the neck up, or are you regularly engaging your heart in support of your life and your service?

Sphere #4: Spirit   Rating (1-10) _____

Sphere #4 explores how connected you feel to something outside of and bigger than yourself. It also explores the sense of inner divinity, the idea that we each are living expressions of a unique, divine seed planted within. There's no dogma implied in this assessment. Whatever your spiritual beliefs, whether they be religious or otherwise, please rate how connected you feel to the spiritual ideas that are relevant and meaningful to you. Do you believe in some organizing energy / spirit / power that connects all things? Do you believe in a connection between people, or between people and the rest of creation? Do you seek or receive some sense of inspiration, clarity, support, and solace from external sources? Do you feel a connection with nature or animals? When you look at the sky, do you feel a sense of wonder and amazement? Do you sense that you have an Inner Gift to share with others? Do any of these elements play a role in how you live or how you serve? If so, how much? Again, there are no right or wrong answers with any of this, simply what is true for you right now. On a scale of 1 to 10, please rate how you would assess your current spiritual self.

Sphere #5: Energy   Rating (1-10) _____

Some people choose to view energy as a component of either their physical self or their spiritual self. I actually see it as both, and also deserving of a category all its own. In talking with Difference Makers, it's been clear to me that many feel worn out, exhausted, overwhelmed, or energetically spent. How would you rate your overall energy level? Do you feel like you have plenty of energy to get through the day and contribute in the way you would like? Does your energy feel focused or scattered? Is your energy natural, or is it largely fueled by caffeine or other influences? Do you tend to feel that you share positive energy or negative energy? Do you feel that your energy is fairly balanced throughout your body? Do you sense spiritual energy flowing to and through you? Are you satisfied with your natural level or energy, or would you like to have more energy to commit to those things that matter most to you?

Sphere #6: Voice   Rating (1-10) _____

How do you use your voice, or your self-expression, to support your cause and to advocate for yourself or your family in your life? Do you easily speak your mind, or do you find that you bite your tongue for fear of saying something others might not want to hear? Do you have a filter for what you say, or do words flow swiftly without much forethought to how they might be perceived by the listener? Do you constantly interrupt to make your point, or do you patiently wait for others to stop speaking and find that you lose your opportunity to voice your opinions? Do you feel that what you have to contribute is meaningful? If something is truly important to you, will you make it known to others? Do you have a regular outlet for expressing yourself, either in conversation, in a journal, or through some other means? Please rate from 1 to 10 how you exercise your voice.

Sphere #7: Resources   Rating (1-10) _____
(Time/Money)

Sphere 7 explores how abundant or lacking you feel resources are in your life. The idea of resources can be expansive and may hold particular meaning for you. Many Difference Makers tell me that time and money are the two resources most on their minds or that bring them the most discomfort. So let's go there. How is your relationship with money and/or time? Do you feel that you have plenty of both to meet your needs? Do you feel like you are the master of your time and money, or do you feel more like their slave? Regardless of where we find ourselves on the income or time scale, our relationship to and how we feel about time and money can impact many facets of our life. Some people can face the money/time relationship head-on. For others, we bury our head in the sand and keep struggling. Please rate from 1 to 10 how you view your relationship with your resources.

Sphere #8: Community/Support   Rating (1-10) _____

As John Donne reminded us, "No man is an island unto himself." We are on this third rock from the sun together, with the opportunity to interact and support each other. In Sphere #8, we look at how you assess your sense of community. Do you feel like there are people in your life who have your back? Do you feel like you are an accepted and welcome part of a group? Do you feel like you have allies in support of your cause or the difference you seek to make? Are there people pulling for you and eager to see you succeed? Do you feel like you are going it alone and have little help or involvement from others? Do you feel like you are good at encouraging and supporting others? How do you rate your current level of community and overall support?

I have never worked with a client who gave themselves perfect tens in each of these eight spheres. Typically, we all have work that can be done in at least one area, or maybe even all of them, that would improve and enhance the way we show up in the world, give to our cause, and enjoy our life. Again, as with all things in this book, do not take any of this as an invitation or opportunity to beat yourself up. Self-awareness is a starting place. We are simply assessing where you are so you can find opportunities to serve with more Real. Big. Love. and to show up as your best and fullest self.

In Chapter 12, we explore ideas and opportunities to invest in these eight spheres so that you can offer Soulful Service from a full teapot.

SOULFUL SERVICE CONSIDERATIONS:

Did anything surprise you in your ratings?

Did one or more areas jump out to you as being particularly in need of your attention?

Is there an area in which improvement in that particular sphere would have positive ripple effects for the other areas?

How do you feel about the idea of serving from your whole, full, Big self?

> *"In every community there is work to be done.*
> *In every nation, there are wounds to heal.*
> *In every heart, there is the power to do it."*
>
> ~ Marianne Williamson

Part 3: LOVE

SOULFUL SERVICE IS DRIVEN BY LOVE:

- Soulful Service asks that we lead with Love, not fear, in our service to others and the world.

- Soulful Service invites us to recognize the inherent value of those we serve, despite circumstance, label, difference, or choices.

- Soulful Service requires us to love and care for ourselves with the same compassion and commitment that we care for others.

- Soulful Service, driven by Love, can change a life and the world.

CHAPTER 10

Love Them Where They Are, Mess and All

In the world of service, as in life, things can be messy. Life happens. Choices are made. Opportunities come and often go. People get down, sometimes stuck. Policies and laws are enacted that hurt rather than help. People who claim to be part of the solution aren't. Greed can overpower compassion. Hate and fear can overpower love.

Let's make a pact not to be a part of that and not to let it get us down. On our watch, let's commit to be the Difference Makers who lead with Love. Let's be the Difference Makers who honor and respect those we serve, not judge and diminish them. Let's lift up our causes and the lives they touch, rather than allow the divisions propagated by fear and greed to become deeper and more ingrained. If we are going to be Difference Makers, let's do it with heart and serve the world with Real. Big. Love.

That's what our causes need. That's what the people and animals and issues and planet we serve long for, even if they don't know it.

When Cynde's son Joe returned from active duty in Iraq, the enormous toll the war had taken on him wasn't immediately obvious. Two weeks after high school graduation, Joe had joined the US Army Reserves. In 2003, he deployed to Iraq as an active, healthy, full-of-life young man, and came back in 2006 with what would later be diagnosed as debilitating PTSD and depression, and a host of other physical and mental challenges. Cynde and her husband Jim now care for Joe in their home. While they are ever hopeful, it may be unlikely that Joe will live independently.

It's been incredibly hard. The sadness of watching a child so changed by the horrors of war is bad enough. But for Cynde, helping her son navigate the confusing military and Veterans Affairs process to find the help he needed added another layer of grueling frustration. She learned that returning vets, especially those facing challenges, are ill-equipped to proactively manage all the paperwork and hurdles that must be cleared before help is even an option.

If Cynde, a licensed professional counselor with three degrees, found the bureaucratic process difficult to navigate, no doubt other veterans and their caregiver families do too.

Her son is not the same—and yet she loves him exactly as he is. It is out of this love for her son and compassion for other families of returning veterans that Cynde founded the Veterans' Families United Foundation in 2007. This nonprofit organization seeks to support the caregiver families of US veterans by connecting them with a network of health-, education-, and empowerment-based tools. Cynde learned the hard way, and now hopes to make the road toward healing less treacherous for others.

For her leadership in bringing support to other caregiver families, Cynde was named the 2018 Elizabeth Dole Foundation Oklahoma Fellow. Asked what she wishes other people knew about military caregivers, Cynde responds, "The tremendous love we have for the veterans in our life. That we, too, leave no one behind."

Authentic, courageous, and consistent love can support and improve a single life as well as pave a more graceful path for many others. Love may not be able to heal all the wounds, but it can ease the pain, aid a community, and help heal the soul.

Let's love people and creation for their own inherent worth and honor them as being inherently worthy, even when—especially when—they may not see or believe it themselves.

The "Namaste" concept that many in the US first encounter in a yoga class can set the stage for this type of interaction. The Sanskrit word, loosely translated, means, "The Divine Light in me recognizes and honors the Divine Light in you." When we choose to look beyond the labels and honor those we serve, those walls of fear and division begin to crumble and often quickly collapse.

Whether teaching in the prisons, working with people in poverty, helping others learn to read, or trying to manage unruly kids, coming back to this grounding notion of Namaste helps me get beyond the superficial distinctions and remember the core of why I serve.

Don't get me wrong, some people are a freaking challenge. They might push all your buttons, get on your last nerve, try to con and deceive you. Some people are dangerous. I'm not suggesting that you drop your guard and be completely trusting. I am proposing that if you want to make a real difference, you have a better chance of doing that if you approach your service from a place of shared humanity and potential empowerment.

Practically, how do we do that?

It's no different with those we serve than with our colleagues, friends, and loved ones. We treat others with compassion and respect.

- Listen. Really listen to what they communicate, both verbally and nonverbally. Feeling heard can be powerful and healing.
- Be present and focused on the interaction, not distracted by devices or a million other thoughts.
- Be patient and give them appropriate time to share and feel heard. Trust me, I know that some people can take advantage of your patience, but until it's clear they are doing that, give folks a chance to be heard.

- Work to listen without judgment and without immediately jumping to fix, counsel, or help with the situation. If we are in a role that expects us to offer guidance, that's one thing, but if we come off with an ego-based need to show we know the "right way" or to spout our opinions, we drive a wedge rather than build a bridge.

Ultimately, Soulful Service is an opportunity to be Love in action. When we serve from the heart, "love" becomes a verb. In addition to a feeling or a way of being, it's a way of acting too. Compassionate listening is one way of demonstrating Love.

"My goal is to educate and lift others up. Education should be that thing that lifts all boats," says Dr. Doug Masterson, a chemistry professor and Associate Provost at the University of Southern Mississippi.

His approach to teaching has transformed over time. A chemist who admits he was originally in it for the research, Doug shifted to a more student-centered perspective after a student commented that he "stood behind a podium and preached."

"That hit me hard," he remembers. "I changed up my style completely." Instead of a podium, he now uses a slide presenter, an Expo marker, and a clip-on microphone, and he walks around throughout class interacting with the students.

"I went from, 'I'm a professor here to do research,' to 'I'm here to help you.' Students pick up on that." Now, his classes enjoy high participation and attendance rates because students know they will get far more in class than the book can provide.

To some, changing a lecture style might not seem like an act of Love. But it is. It shows a willingness to listen, a willingness to put the needs of others before our own ego, a willingness to be open to our own change so that we can better help others change.

Teaching. Showing. Being present. Facilitating growth. Asking questions to help others find their own answers and giving them the space and respect to do so. Ultimately, serving with Love means showing up, allowing others to be exactly where they are, and for that to be okay. Then we grow from there.

When you can do that, you often grow just as much if not more than those you serve. You are able to be open to the growth, rather than building walls against it. In doing so, you can encourage others to be Real and Big, too.

Love in service is not always easy. It can be heartbreaking. It can be frustrating. People can try to take advantage of kindness.

Sharon enjoyed her job at a shelter serving at-risk girls. The girls there had faced significant trauma or drama in their lives, and that often came out in the way they interacted with the staff. For Sharon, the job was rewarding, and also incredibly challenging. Without compassion for what the girls had been through, strong boundaries and clear rules, and the mutual support of the other staff members, it would not have been sustainable. Even though their actions often made it hard, she had to genuinely care about the girls and have a sense of optimism about helping them envision and create a more positive future.

To look out for yourself, you need to have clear boundaries. Boundaries are important for your own self-care, and to ensure that others are not becoming dependent. Enabling and fostering dependency does those you serve no favors.

Holding people accountable is ultimately a sign of respect. Accountability is an indication that you think enough about the other person to believe that they can make progress, follow the rules, contribute to their own success. Boundaries and accountability give others the opportunity to be the Difference Makers in their own lives.

Love can build people up and help them find the confidence and strength to make progress. However, as much as I would like to believe differently, Love is not a panacea. The absence of Love can create problems, but the presence of Love can't solve all problems. This recognition is not meant to stop you from being loving, rather to serve as a reminder that, no matter how much you care, some outcomes are outside your control.

Coop learned the hard way that love and presence aren't always enough to prevent unfortunate outcomes with his students. Although at times heartbreaking, an important shift in thinking helps him now find that the rewards outweigh the pain.

"We all deserve a chance," Coop says. "Tell me one person who hasn't made some major mistake in life. I want to make a difference. My approach is to love them (the students) until they can learn to love themselves."

Despite the tough, rugged exterior he presents, Coop credits a 12-step program and solo excursions into the forest with helping him open his heart and be able and willing to access his emotions. When I asked how he deals with the disappointment or heartbreak of the job, the tough exterior crumbled.

This is one example of what we are passionate about and what breaks our heart being two sides of the same coin.

Coop is driven to help teens who have ventured off-course once again find their way. But he's learned that he can't save them all, and that is an incredibly difficult realization. Any student suicide is difficult to accept, but one in particular caused him to doubt his effectiveness and rethink his career choice. This student had access to high-end treatment options and therapy, yet, according to his dad, was most comfortable with Coop. Despite numerous styles, approaches, and treatments, nothing effectively managed his mental illness.

Coop was shattered by the student's suicide. Now, years later, he still gets choked up thinking about it. His big realization: "I can't predict what will happen or save anybody. I can only give what I can give."

In this case, he gave Love. The student's father even asked him to give the eulogy at the teenager's funeral. Coop credits that request with helping him decide to stay with the profession. The family recognized his impact, and he realized that his ability and willingness to be a support for the family in their time of need was also service.

Service isn't always easy. It's also not always life or death. But when unfortunate things happen to people you care about or in a cause you love, it can be a challenge to manage.

It is a loving act to share your gifts. When you do share your gifts, when you lead with what makes your soul sing, you can't choose the outcome. You can hope for an outcome, you can work toward an outcome, but you can't guarantee the outcome. None of us can.

It might feel easier to pack up our gifts and quit trying. But in doing so, we then deny everyone else the opportunity to learn or benefit from them. Walling ourselves off from the pain can inflict even more pain.

Sharing doesn't just come from the heart. When you share from a place of Soulful Service, there's more of you present and able to serve. Even when the heart feels tender, the mind, body, and spirit can rally to keep us moving forward. When Coop's heart was broken, his mind was getting in the way and discouraging service, but it was a new perspective introduced through his spirit that helped him reconsider his service and to continue helping kids.

When we allow our values, our authenticity, our courage, and our consistency to drive our Love based service, we can be more fully present with those we serve and more fully present to our own needs, as well. Serving with Real. Big. Love. helps us offer our best to others, and also care for ourselves as part of the service equation.

SOULFUL SERVICE CONSIDERATIONS:

Do you intentionally lead with Love in your service to others?

Are you able to recognize when judgment potentially hampers service?

How are your boundaries? Are you able to offer Love and be of service while also respecting your own time, energy, and priorities?

How do you manage disappointments or heartbreak with those you serve?

Chapter 11

Love You Where You Are, Mess and All

If we want a more loving world, we begin by being more loving. To be more loving to others, we begin by being more loving to ourselves. For all the big changes we desire in the external world, we begin by changing the quality of our internal world.

Soulful Service is as much an inside job as it is a way of being of service for others.

As Difference Makers, we may not want to hear this. Can't we simply pour our attention into helping others, into saving the outer world, and ignore the messiness of our interior world?

Sorry, friend. It doesn't work that way, or at least it doesn't work that way very well or for very long.

This world needs you. All of you. This world needs your gifts. This world needs your passion and compassion. This world needs your love. This world also needs you to nurture and support and love the precious gift that you are, so that you can bring your best self to your life and your service.

Perfection is not required to be a Difference Maker. In fact, those very things you may see as imperfections could be the bridges that allow you to better reach others.

Coop's history overcoming addiction gives him credibility with the students he reaches. Being diagnosed with breast cancer was a crappy experience, but being a survivor of breast cancer helps my mom connect with her mammogram patients. My own history of being exhausted and overwhelmed while trying to make a difference may be why you are still reading this book. You know that in my own way, I get what you're experiencing.

Some of us serve others as a way to make up for our own lagging self-worth. We might not view ourselves as lovable, so it's easier to heap our love on others. Or perhaps we believe that the only thing about us that is worthy of love is our service.

Soulful Service always begins with you, including how you treat and minister to yourself. What if you agreed with the radical notion of being a bit nicer, gentler, and more supportive to yourself so that you can then better extend that grace to others?

The fact that you want to serve others at all, that you want to make this world a better place, is an indication that you are wholly worthy of your own love. When you are able to genuinely love, appreciate, and accept yourself where you are, you are more open and able to do those things for others too.

I can feel your eye rolls through the page. Enough with the self-love crap, you might be thinking. Before you completely dismiss the idea, let's explore it a bit further.

In her *Psychology Today* article, "A Seven-Step Prescription for Self-Love," Deborah Khoshaba, Psy.D., a clinical psychologist and director of training and development for the Hardiness Institute, defines self-love this way:

Sounds an awful lot like how we seek to serve others. What if we extend to ourselves the very compassion and kindness that we use to reach others or promote our cause?

Yes, self-love can be observed and promoted through our actions, but that's not enough. Let's take a look at our thoughts. How do we talk to and about ourselves, what do we say about ourselves in our own minds?

Beware the Bully Brain

Let me ask it this way: If someone else were to say the things that you say to yourself to your kid, your friend, or your grandma, how would you feel about that? Would it be time to put the smack-down on them?

Yeah, that's what I thought.

When my daughter entered middle school, she began saying unkind things out loud about herself. I had to intervene.

"Don't talk about my daughter that way."

"Mom, give me a break. I'm talking about myself."

"If I wouldn't be okay with other people talking to you that way, why do you think *you* talking to you that way is any better?"

I may have received the standard teenage eye roll and huff with that one, but it sunk in. The very next day, I was berating myself about something, and she chimed in, "Hey, don't talk about my momma like that."

The things we say to ourselves, either in our own minds or aloud, have an effect on our psyche and our overall well-being. Even the Mayo Clinic links negative self-talk with higher levels of depression, poorer cardiovascular health, and decreased life span.

For many of us, our own self-criticism has become such a normal way of life that we hardly notice it anymore. Maggie, a coach who has helped me better understand the power of the Bully Brain, wanted to make the point crystal clear. For one day, she directed the four ladies in our coaching group to place a bean, marble, or small rock in our bra every time we had a negative thought or comment toward ourselves.

Of course, I thought this whole exercise was ridiculous. But my young daughter overhead the phone conversation, and eager for any reason at that age to get to wear a bra, she wanted to play too. By the end of the day, I was much more cognizant of my own self-talk because my bra was filled with beans and my boobs hurt. If one day of beans can cause such discomfort, what kind of pain and discomfort does a lifetime of self-criticism inflict?

What if we put the smack-down on that Bully Brain that has been trash talking us for decades?

But how?

Bookstore shelves are filled with self-help books related to affirmations and changing your mindset. I'd done the research, knew the whys and even some hows, but I wasn't making progress on muzzling that Bully Brain.

Ultimately, I decided that, rather than try to silence the ever-present and talkative Bully Brain, and then beat myself up again when I couldn't, I'd try to drown it out with happier, more helpful thoughts. Again… but how?

I set up a trigger. My birthday is July 23. I decided that every time I saw 7:23 on a digital clock, I would say, "Seven twenty-three, I love me."

Cheesy as hell, I know.

But in that brief moment, I would smile. I started seeing 7:23 on the clock at least twice a day (none of the clocks in my world are set to the same time, so it is possible to catch 7:23 many times throughout the day). Then, 723 would appear in other places: on license plates, in movies, on receipts, and in other random locations. Every time I see it, I think, "Seven twenty-three, I love me." I smile, allow myself to feel happy, and then go on with my day.

Caught in the act, my husband asked one day what I was thinking that made me smile. I took a risk and told him what I was up to. Much to my surprise, he joined in.

Our anniversary happens to be October 23, so every time he sees 10:23, he says, "Ten twenty-three, I love we." It has become a thing. Now, we both randomly glance at the clock or check our phones at 23 minutes after the hour. Texts of screenshots with :23

litter our camera rolls and have become our little love notes to each other throughout the day.

All it took was a trigger to encourage myself to say one nice thing. The one trigger snowballed. Interestingly, the negative self-talk has subsided, and I can genuinely say that I feel happier. Maybe it's just being goofy with the time thing that makes me happier, or that my husband and I now have our own cheesy love note game, but the end result is the same. This one little trigger upped my self-love game.

What could your trigger be? How might you build in kind words to yourself throughout your day? Some clients I work with choose to put positive words on sticky notes and put them in places where they will see them throughout the day—on the sun visor in the car, on a mirror by the door, in the closet by the shoe rack. Others set an alarm on their phone to go off at a certain time to give a little positive word pick-me-up throughout the day.

Part of the Inner Bully game also hinges on feelings of blame, guilt, and shame. Honestly, these do no one any good. If you find that you blame yourself for the woes of the world, that you feel guilty for whatever reason, or that you still experience shame for some past situation, notice that these feelings and thoughts are all choices that you make and that you can replace with something more nourishing.

One technique I've learned through my involvement with ITP (Integral Transformative Practice) is the art of staying current with my feelings. That gives me a chance to see that, when feelings of guilt, shame, or blame arise, they are always rooted in the past. I can do nothing to change the past, so I can notice if I am fine in the present moment (yep, I'm fine), and then I can choose to shift my attention from past stuff that brings me down to present things to appreciate. Again, it's a choice. The first step, though, is to recognize those ways in which guilt, shame, and blame sneak in, and then make the decision that I am worth the effort to change my perspective.

You are the authority in your own life. You have the power and opportunity to not only be responsible for how you show up on in the world, but also for how you show up in your inner world. Self-flagellation with your own thoughts or words does no one any favors. It brings you down. And, when you are down, you are not as available for those you serve.

In talking with a very wise friend and counselor, I once inquired why my relationship at that time was so hard. My friend pointed out that some people love with their hearts, but other people love with their heads. The distance between the two approaches can feel like a huge chasm. This distinction was significant for me. I also realized how it applied not only in the situation of that unhappy relationship, but also in the relationship I had with myself.

We often use our minds to critique, judge, and criticize, and use our hearts for gratitude, appreciation, tenderness, and compassion. When we view ourselves only through the lens of our mind, our self-talk is more likely to be critical. If we can view ourselves through the eyes of our heart, or even the eyes of our soul, then the messages we send ourselves can take on a more beautiful, inspired, uplifted approach.

This is, in essence, Soulful Service toward ourselves.

If we seek to protect ourselves from the compassion fatigue we may experience in serving others, we also need to insulate against the criticism fatigue that we induce in ourselves. Constant negative chatter about yourself drains your energy and leaves you feeling flat.

Forgiveness Is Freeing

Granted, you are not the only one who may wrong you or act in a way that is hurtful. If you have people in your life, then you likely deal with emotional drama and pain. That's part of the human dance. Again, you get to choose whether you hold onto, react, or release pain that is instigated by others.

Over the course of the past couple of years, I've had the opportunity to put this understanding to the test.

To say that my dad and I have had a strained relationship throughout my life would be an enormous understatement. After a couple of attempts to make it work, my parents divorced when I was eight and my younger brother was four. I saw my dad only on often-dreaded and occasional weekend, holiday, and summer visits. When I moved to Washington, D.C. after college, I was relieved to have a good 17-hour car drive between us.

After his fifth divorce, life got rough for Dad. Hanging out with sketchy people, poor choices, and decades of terrible health and drinking caught up to him. And he needed a place to live.

With no other options, and after a persuasive phone call from his sister, I hesitantly arranged for Dad to move the five hours from his boyhood hometown to a community near me.

This terrified me. Not to sound too dramatic, but I feared that the peace of my new marriage and my own sanity were about to be upended by inviting back into my life the one person who is my equivalent of an emotional tornado.

I had a choice to make.

I could hold onto every hurt from the past four decades and make us both miserable.

Or, I could choose to interact with my dad from a place of love, rather than a place of judgment and resentment.

I choose love. Every time I feel myself wanting to judge, I view it as an invitation to love him more. And the truth is, it's absolutely the most loving thing I could do for myself too.

As much as I feared moving him nearby, it turns out that it's been the thing that has healed those decades of distance and pain. I'm grateful for the opportunity to have a new chance at this old relationship.

As Louis Smedes wrote, "To forgive is to set a prisoner free and discover that the prisoner was you."

Forgiveness isn't easy. It doesn't mean forgetting. It doesn't even mean accepting. Forgiveness is making a conscious choice to not continue to be saddled with the emotional baggage of someone else's bad choices. Free yourself from those chains.

And, if you are the one who made the bad choices that need to be forgiven, give yourself that gift too. Feel the feeling. Learn the lesson. Forgive yourself. Move forward from a wiser, more compassionate place.

It might be that seeking the guidance of a trained therapist or counselor can help enormously to untangle those chains of the past. If you have deeply held, stuck resentment and anger that impede your ability to live forward with grace and freedom, then by all means make yourself enough of a priority to get the help you might need to set yourself free.

Forgiveness is the ultimate act of love for ourselves.

If we are to keep our teapot filled, we have to ensure that we are not the ones draining it dry through negative self-talk, resentments, and self-defeating habits. The demands of the world and of our service are enough to try to counteract through self-care, it makes no sense to increase the burden through our own choice to be a pain in our own ass.

Replace These Three Rs to Experience Greater Peace

Much like the three F-Bombs that can obstruct our Big service, there are three Rs that can act like roadblocks to our inner peace: Resentment, Regret, and Resistance.

Resentment is that mixture of anger, disappointment, and fear that can cast heavy shade on even our sunniest days. Defined as "bitter indignation at being treated unfairly," resentment is a particularly —unhelpful state of mind. As many have said, resentment is like drinking poison and waiting for the other person to die. It doesn't change the situation, and it doesn't change another person. It only pollutes our energy.

When we cling to resentment we continue to give our power away to the person or situation we resent. That just sucks. The last thing we want to do is give them the chance to continue messing with our lives and our heads. Instead, we are doing it for them.

Let's drop resentment like the hot, burning coal that it is.

Regret can also weigh us down. This feeling of disappointment, of missing out, and mourning something done or not done in the past can cause us to get caught in the shoulda, woulda, coulda mental spin cycle. There's nothing at all productive about that.

We can't change the past, so holding ourselves hostage to it is a sure-fire recipe for negative self-talk and diminished peace. As Katherine Mansfield said, "Regret is an appalling waste of energy, you can't build on it—it's only good for wallowing in." If you've done something you truly regret, you can work to make amends or to make peace in your own mind. Only through a major shift in thinking about the circumstance can we also shift our feelings from regret to something more productive.

Sometimes it's not what we did do, but what we failed to do that haunts us the most. Adventure author Rafael Sabatini wrote, "Regret of neglected opportunity is the worst hell that a living soul can inhabit." While that sounds pretty dramatic, the toll it can take on our mental health is significant.

This kind of regret can often be the by-product of the third painful R: Resistance.

Resistance is when we prevent ourselves from moving forward toward a bigger, more meaningful future that is more aligned with our soul. In my own life and with my clients, I've seen that the very thing that would make the biggest positive difference in our lives or our service is also the very thing we most resist.

Often the prize might exist right outside our comfort zone, so we resist the action necessary to reach it. This is one more expression of fear and unhelpful "what ifs"—what if I'm not good enough, what if people don't like it or me, what if I try and fail, what if I succeed and my world changes....

In working with my own coach, she often encourages that the thing I resist the most is the thing I must do. That's the key to my next opportunity for evolution and contribution. That's the narrow passage of my Soulful Service.

It's true that what we resist persists, at least as that uncomfortable niggling in the back of our mind of what could be. The path to uncovering our true potential is punctuated by resistance. Will that punctuation be a full-stop period, the pause of a comma, or the exclamation point of feeling the resistance and moving forward anyway? I root for the latter.

When we experience Resentment, Regret, or Resistance, it's a clear indication that we are not living in the present. The past is haunting us, or the potential of the future is scaring us. By focusing on the present, it's easier to drop these peace-stealers in order to better care for our minds, our hearts, and our positive contribution.

Behold the Power of Gratitude

One additional way you can counteract both the three Rs and the Bully Brain is through the magic and healing power of gratitude.

In her own beautiful, direct fashion, one of my favorite authors, Anne Lamott, lights the way for more joy in our lives:

"Gratitude and service are the two best paths to joy. I mean, I'm not stupid—if you want loving feelings, do loving things. Period."

There you have it. You already do loving things. You are halfway there!

The power of gratitude does have the ability to shift our perspective, help us appreciate even the tiny things that are right in the present moment, and usher in more of the qualities for which we are grateful.

I'm often humbled when people who seemingly have so little can find gratitude for the most interesting things.

Much to the annoyance of each new college class I teach at the prisons, every week I ask students to share one thing new or good that has happened to them since we last met. At first, they think I'm nuts. "You realize we're locked up, right, Mrs. Berry? There's not a damn thing good in here, and every day is the same."

Okay, I hear you. But you took a breath this morning, right? Can you see that as good?

You get the point.

From this one simple activity, I've been amazed to see how much easier it is for the students to find something positive to share and how more positive experiences flow their way. People who haven't had visits or letters in years may start receiving them. Some students begin to stay out of trouble and stay sober, which is apparently harder to do in prison than I realized. Some experience improved relations with family. Many report hope for a better life upon release and a more positive outlook in general.

When we focus on the good, it seems we generate more good to focus on.

One Monday, a student bubbled over with excitement. She reported that for the first time in 17 years, she was able to purchase a bag of chips at the prison canteen. A bag of chips. Given her genuine reaction, it could have been a golden tiara, a cure to cancer, or a trip to Disney World. It was a bag of chips, something most of us would take for granted, and it brought her enormous joy.

When we are able to find joy in the little things, finding joy in the big things comes easier too. When we can't find something for which to be grateful, it's hard to find joy in anything.

I'm a firm believer that gratitude works. Rumor has it that Oprah has kept a daily gratitude journal for more than three decades. Granted, it might seem that finding things to be grateful for is probably pretty easy for her. That said, if my prison students can do it, I know you can too.

Even when times are bleak, we all have things for which we can be grateful. Remembering that and allowing those positive feelings to wash over us is another quick, easy, and free tool to bring out joy and show love to ourselves.

Bookstores and the internet are flooded with resources to help us learn to love ourselves more or be more compassionate toward ourselves. But no volume of research, not even the golden ticket of self-help, can make a difference until we believe we are worthy of our own care, compassion, and love—until we can recognize the blessings all around us and be grateful for them, big and small.

If you have any doubt, let me tell you right now, you are worthy.

Now give yourself a hug, and let's put this self-care business into practice.

SOULFUL SERVICE CONSIDERATIONS:

In what ways do you act toward or speak to yourself that are unkind or unhelpful?

Is your brain a bully?
What triggers might you employ to shift toward more positive, uplifting conversation in your own mind?

Are Regret or Resentment weighing you down?
Are you ready/willing to let them go in an act of self-love?

What are you resisting?
Could a path of more Soulful Service exist on the other side of your Resistance?

CHAPTER 12

Soulful Self-Care Strategies for Bringing the Love

I love unexpected surprise gifts from the Universe. Having just opened up the document to begin writing this chapter, my husband brings me my phone because the text notification had sounded. One of my new clients sent a picture of the quote for today from her *You Are a Badass* tear-off desk calendar.

> *"You aren't a selfish person for taking care of yourself, just a happier one. Take care of yourself as if you are the most awesome person you've ever met."*
>
> ~Jen Sincero

There you have it, Difference Maker. You can be a Badass for your cause, and you can also be a happier, more effective Badass by taking care of you. A Soulful Badass. I like it.

In talking with Difference Makers, I ask what they do regularly to take care of themselves. I'm normally greeted with one of four responses:

1. I'm too damn busy taking care of the rest of the world to have the time or money to take care of me. Besides, that would be selfish.

2. I exercise regularly, or at least sometimes.
3. I get a massage or get my nails done on occasion.
4. I try to meditate some.

By now, you probably have a good sense about how I feel about answer number 1. Hello, teapot. But what about the other three answers?

I applaud any effort you take to care for yourself. Thank you for looking out for you. That said, self-care efforts focused exclusively in one area do not lead to Soulful Service. You are more than just your body or your mind or your fingernails. This is in no way an effort to detract from the four-times-a-week CrossFitter or the twice-a-day meditator. It's simply an observation that, while exercise or meditation do indeed have positive effects on our lives, we have other areas that also need our attention if we are to be truly kind to ourselves. With a broader focus on how you care for yourself, you are more likely to show up as the best, fullest version of yourself so you can make your biggest difference.

We are going to break down each of the Eight Spheres of Soulful Self-Care and offer ideas and opportunities to nurture and care for these particular areas of your life.

Here's the deal: I am not encouraging you to even think about doing everything listed in each category below. They are simply ideas. You may already be doing some or even many of these things. If so, YEA YOU!

And I'm not suggesting that you feel the need to do something in every category. This isn't about guilting you or wearing you out even more. My hope is that you come across a couple of ideas in more than one category that feel nurturing and like something that you could incorporate regularly into your routine.

The Eight Spheres assessment in Chapter 8 gave you insight into areas that could most benefit from your attention. You also chose one area in particular that could benefit the most. Keep your assessment in mind as you make your way through this list. The key with any of these is to find something that you enjoy, that you can commit to, and that makes a difference for you.

When working with clients, I ask them to begin by identifying at least one tactic in three or four categories that there's a reasonable chance they would consistently integrate into their regular routine. In the area they identify as their biggest opportunity, we may pick a couple of tactics. In some areas, they may already be doing things regularly that support them, so we celebrate those and stick with them. We get creative about combining ideas or thinking about how to add them in to a regular part of the day so that the self-care efforts can help them breathe easier rather than cause anxiety.

Body

Our physical bodies are amazing! Regardless of the size, shape, flexibility, or condition they are in, our bodies are remarkable and miraculous vehicles for driving our contributions in the world. When you tend to your body with care and intention, you can increase your physical energy, stamina, and ability to be of service. This has nothing to do with aesthetics or how you look, and everything to do with how you feel and the capacity you have to engage in the world.

- **Move your body regularly.** On purpose. With intention. Let the energy in your body have an outlet to be released rather than stagnate. Interestingly, doing so helps usher in more fresh energy. How you move your body is less important than that you simply do it, regularly, in a form, at a pace, and for a duration that works for where you are now.
- **Listen to your body.** It is wise, with much to tell you. Once you listen, actually follow its advice.
- **Breathe.** Really. Don't sniff at the air, actually inhale and deeply exhale. Do this on purpose several times throughout the day.

- **Get outside and in nature.** Vitamin D and fresh air do the body (and the spirit) good.
- **Laugh!** Big belly laughs are good for the soul, and they are my favorite ab workout.
- **Sleep.** This is admittedly the most difficult for me personally. That said, ample science backs up the importance of regular, good-quality, and quantity sleep. We do function better physically, mentally, and emotionally when we are regularly well-rested.
- **Fuel up with better nutrition.** Feed your body what it needs. Notice how different foods make your body feel. Food is fuel, and we benefit when we can treat it as such. My body has told me loud and clear to lay off the sugar and flour. When I listen and follow my body's wisdom, it works better, and I feel better.
- **Push your body.** Challenge it. When we increase our physical potential and the boundaries of what is possible, we boost our confidence. The body is an amazing, miraculous machine. When we have a bit of confidence in it, we can often blow our own minds.
- **Rest when you need to.** In addition to sleep, you need some periods of rest and relaxation. Don't push until you wear yourself out. Give yourself permission to simply rest when you need to.
- **Body work.** A good old massage, reflexology, salt-water float, or energy treatment can do wonders for the body. Some people call this pampering, but I believe it also helps release stale energy and can be healing for the body.

Mind

Our minds are such magnificent tools for moving us and our contribution forward. Sometimes the mind can be a real pain in the ass too. Our opportunity is to lead and engage the mind to work with us rather than against us, to help us harness courage for progress, rather than fear and resistance. When we pay attention to the quality of the conversation in our own head, we can enhance our outlook and our attitude.

- **Never stop learning.** Learning doesn't stop when we leave high school. Learning is a lifelong activity that invigorates our curiosity, broadens our perspective, and allows us to keep growing. I truly believe that when we stop learning, we start dying, and we've got too much good to do for that! Learn, baby, learn. Go grow your brain!
- **Teach others.** It's a great way to serve and to integrate your own learning even more. This doesn't have to be in a classroom or formal setting. Sharing your ideas, skills, hobbies, and insight with others can take place in a wide variety of ways.
- **Notice your thoughts.** Notice the Bully Brain. Take care to intentionally shift your thoughts from hurtful to more helpful ones. The resource section at the back of this book highlights some effective tools that can help with this. This is something I also work on with clients. If needed, therapy can also be an option for reframing unhelpful thinking.
- **Engage in fear-busting.** Recognize and list your fears—anything that may be holding you back from Big service, and then use your mind to analyze and shift those fearful thoughts. Fear can paralyze. Awareness can be freeing.
- **Plan and prioritize.** Use the power of your mind positively and proactively to plan and prioritize where you will invest your time and energy for greatest impact. I spend a lot of time here with clients. We look to their values and roles in developing goals for the year, month, and week, and then engage those beautiful minds in actually doing the work to accomplish the goals.

- **Recite affirmations.** Develop affirmations that can help reset your mind and seed it with positivity and possibility. Affirmations are a great touchstone and a quick way to muzzle the Bully Brain.
- **Get stuff done.** Avoid the mental constipation of things left undone. This is like clutter of the mind. Work in a focused way to get things completed, delegate them, or take them off the to-do list. Don't let the undone hang over your head like a rain cloud.

Heart

In the Body, Mind, Soul movement, I've been dismayed at the lack of specific attention offered to the heart. Our hearts are *amazing* and powerful as tools both for circulation and transformation. Our hearts may be what motivates us to feel so deeply for our cause or the difference we want to make in the world. Our why is often driven by the feeling in our heart. I believe our hearts are where that Inner Spark resides, the place where Spirit and Matter meet, the heart of Soulful Service. The heart deserves and needs our nurturing attention.

- **Gratitude.** Seriously, y'all. This is so powerful. Consider a gratitude journal and daily write out and acknowledge what you are grateful for. My client Hillary keeps a gratitude jar at home for the family to fill throughout the year with colorful notes of gratitude. At the end of the year, she reads through each one before emptying the jar to begin again the next year. This can be done at work as well. Much like the "New and Goods" during my classes at the prisons, you might be surprised at how the act of gratefully recognizing the good in life can have an amazing way of ushering in more to be grateful for.
- **Write in a journal.** This is one of my very favorite ways to open my heart and express my feelings. Write it out. Let

your heart flow through your pen. Interestingly, if you are dealing with something troubling, the act of writing it out can diffuse some of the power of those negative emotions. Journals are also a great place to celebrate good things and accomplishments and joys (big or little) in your life. Simply silence the inner critic and acknowledge your feelings on the paper.

- **Forgive.** For your benefit, not theirs. Release the emotional hold that old hurts have on you and reclaim that emotional energy. This is a powerful practice for clearing the energy of the heart to make room for happier, more satisfying feelings to come in.
- **Stay current.** If you find that you are having regrets about or dwelling in the past, or worrying about the future, come back to right now. Typically, in this very moment, all is well, and you are fine. Staying current allows us to get out of our head and enjoy peace that we can find in our heart.
- **Talk it out.** Clear the air. This is also relevant under Sphere #6 for voice. Holding feelings in, trying to ignore or suppress them, creates a slippery slope that makes us sick and steals our power. Sphere #7 for community can be helpful in giving you a safe space to share your concerns. If you need a counselor, by all means get one. Taking good care of your heart, of your emotional self, matters.
- **Invest in relationships that nurture you.** As a Difference Maker, you may seek out or find yourself in relationships where you serve others. Make sure you have some relationships that also nurture and support, rather than drain, you.
- **Engage in heart-based meditations.** Some guided or sound-driven meditations are intended to help open, clear, and activate the power and intelligence of your heart. For more information, visit the HeartMath Institute online.

Spirit

This is the home of our true inspiration and our Inner Spark, or unique gift, that we have to offer the world. To be truly effective and empowering, spiritual attention can't be exclusively externally focused. By exploring our inner spirit and infusing it in and with our heart, we can step into the very nature of Love-driven Soulful Service. And you can insure that you extend the essence and the blessing of Soulful Service to yourself, so that you can more fully extend it to others.

- **Pray.** Every person, every religious belief, approaches prayer in a different way. I've often heard people say, "I don't know how to pray right." What if there is no right or wrong way, simply our way? Just be willing to have a conversation with the Divine. As Meister Eckhart once said, "If the only prayer you ever said was thank you, that would be enough."
- **Seek to recognize and appreciate the interconnectedness of all things.** There's a Divine grace in the connection between all things. When we begin to see and understand this, and our role in the bigger picture, it can inspire us to add more meaningfully and positively to the greater whole by taking good care of ourselves and showing up fully. Again, this is the foundation of Soulful Service.
- **Reconnect with nature.** For some, spending time in nature is when they feel the closest to Spirit, the most inspired, the most at peace. When we enjoy the beauty of creation outside ourselves, we would do well to appreciate the beauty of creation that we are too.
- **Read, watch, or listen to uplifting material.** There's no shortage of media available in the world. Regularly choose to interact with books, movies, music, or podcasts that uplift your spirit. And try to reduce the amount of time and energy you invest in material that dampens or darkens your spirit.
- **Meditate.** Some people view meditation as a "mindfulness"

activity. I view it more as opening the door to the other side of the conversation with Spirit. When we pray, we talk to the Divine. When we meditate, we give Spirit a chance to talk back. We can learn much if we will work to quiet our minds and be open to what Spirit has to say.

- **Look for and embrace the Namaste.** Find the Namaste, the Divine Light, that connects us, especially with those who are a challenge. When we can recognize and honor the Divine Light in ourselves and others, that opens the door to serving from the soul.
- **Find a spiritual community that is a good fit for you and engage.** This may or may not be the spiritual community of our youth. This may or may not be an official organization with a specific way of believing. As someone who considers myself spiritual, but not necessarily religious, living in the Bible Belt, I've had to get creative to find and engage in a spiritual community of open-minded, big-hearted people. Feeling encouraged and supported to explore our spiritual beliefs with others can be an important part of our own growth.
- **Listen to your intuition.** Intuitive hunches, just knowing, feelings, etc. are Spirit's way of communicating with us throughout our everyday existence, not just when we are in an elusive state of Zen. Don't discount coincidences or gut feelings. Notice when your soul sings. Listen for guidance and encouragement and reassurance from Spirit. Recognize that goose bumps and tingly sensations may be more than an indication you need a sweater. They may be messages from the Divine.
- **Grow your understanding.** Continue to learn and expand your spiritual perspective as a way to remain aligned and grow in spiritual ways. Some people allow their beliefs to stagnate after being told what or how to believe in their

youth. There's so much more richness and texture and meaning to explore throughout all phases of our lives.

Energy

Ahhhhh, energy. When we are feeling exhausted and overwhelmed, energy seems to be in short supply. Or it may come to us in bursts—the fight-or-flight kind of adrenaline hits that get us through the next big situation. Or, for some of us, the energy we rely on is thanks to yet another cup of coffee or caffeine fix that keeps us chugging along.

Energy is about much more than just the physical fuel we have to engage and get through the day. It's also about the quality or vibe of our interactions with others; with ourselves; with Spirit. Of all the eight spheres, energy is the one for me that infuses and feeds or smothers and detracts from all the others.

The quality of our energy reveals the quality of our life and our service.

In my view of life, energy is everywhere, and it enlivens everything. When we "get a vibe" from people, that's energy talking. When we feel effervescent inside from excitement, that's energy talking. When we are with some people and feel like they are sucking the life force right out of us, that's energy talking.

Taking care of your energy is about more than simply the physical elements of sleep, exercise, hydration, and nutrition. Those are critically important, of course. It's also about being intentional about the energy we let in and that we put out. Even if this is a foreign concept for you, hang in with me here. When we understand more about how we are affected by the energy in and around us, and how to make more energy available to us, our lives and our service can radically change for the better.

- **Hydrate.** Yes, drinking water improves energy levels. Studies have found that even mild dehydration can alter a person's energy level, mood, and ability to think clearly. Next time you hit that mid-afternoon slump, drink a big

glass of water rather than grab a pop or candy bar. Being consistently well-hydrated helps us feel more energized.
- **Sleep.** This is a bit of a no-brainer. Operating on too little sleep throws our energy off. During sleep, our energy reserves replenish. We recharge. When we sleep too little, or we sleep poorly, our energy lags the next day. Make sleep a priority.
- **Enjoy energizing foods.** Real, unprocessed foods that are rich in vitamins and minerals naturally support our energy levels. Processed foods that are filled with sugar and chemicals deplete our energy levels. When I know I need to keep my energy up during the workday, I have learned to avoid refined carbs at lunch. They send me straight to Snoozeville. While everyone may react differently to foods, it's becoming more commonly accepted that proteins and even fats will offer more consistent, longer-term energy than the bump-and-dip energy of carbs.
- **Consider your supplements.** If you notice that your energy feels remarkably low, you might talk with your doctor about checking your vitamin levels. Low levels of D or B vitamins, as well as low magnesium, antioxidants, or Omega-3, can result in less energy and an overall sluggish feeling.
- **Energy breaks.** The days of smoke breaks have nearly gone the way of the dinosaur, and in their place, more people are turning to energy breaks. This is simply a chance to stand, to stretch, to get a glass of water, or to take a quick walk. Really, it's anything that will help amp up your energy, especially if you've been sitting in front of a computer for an extended period. Many fitness trackers now come equipped with alerts that go off once an hour to remind wearers to get up and move around.
- **Breathe deep.** Taking in adequate oxygen through our

breathing improves energy levels. Many of us breath shallowly, and the full benefit of oxygen doesn't fully reach our system. Deeper, slower breaths can force more oxygen into our cells, helping us to feel more energized and less zapped throughout the day. Consider setting an alarm on your phone for twice a day as a reminder to consciously take ten or more deep, full, slow breaths. It takes less than two minutes, and you will feel a boost of energy afterward.

- **Practice good energy hygiene—ground and clear.** It's safe to say that we all take showers, brush our teeth, and, hopefully, use deodorant. Regular hygiene is important for our bodies, and it's important for our energy too. We are like energetic sponges, picking up energy, both uplifting and depleting, from all around us. Just as we wouldn't want grime and germs hanging around on our skin, we don't want to carry around negative, unhelpful energy either. Making a point of clearing and removing stagnate, unhelpful, even hurtful energy from your body, mind, heart, and spirit can help bolster your own energy and keep you from being dragged down by the energy of others. Even taking a cool shower or immersing in a salt bath can help clear out the energy of others.

- **Practice energetic protection or shielding.** We can protect ourselves from absorbing negative, unhelpful, or depleting energy around us. Energetic shielding is a process by which you set an intention to create a boundary around you that is impervious to the energy of others. You might consider it like wearing a cloak or being encompassed in a beautiful bubble of light. Your mind is like a magic wand when it comes to energy, so imagine anything that is meaningful and uplifting to you. The energy of big crowds tends to weird me out, so I image being surrounded by an egg shape filled with white light. I set the intention that only energies of love, gratitude, or peace are able to get in or out of the egg. When we are in service, especially in tough circumstances, this one energy hack can help us stay true to our own energy without relinquishing it or taking on energetic baggage throughout the day.

- **Try Eastern methods for moving energy through the body.** For centuries, Eastern cultures have appreciated the importance of energy as the fuel for our human form and also as the connection with the Divine. Modalities like Qigong, Tai Chi, acupressure, and acupuncture all seek to improve the flow of energy throughout the body via the energy meridian system. These methods seek to clear energy blockages and stimulate the system so energy can flow more easily throughout the body.

- **Work with your chakras.** We can thank our friends in the East for introducing us to the chakra system. The primary seven chakras are energy centers, or spinning wheels, in the body from the base of the spine to the crown of the head. No, you can't see them on an x-ray, and as a result, many people in the West claim that they therefore don't exist. But as someone who has worked extensively with my own chakra system and interacted with brilliant colleagues who have too, I can tell you that learning about, engaging with, and keeping your chakra system open and clear does enhance energy, clarity, connectivity, and productivity.

- **Try essential oils.** Essential oils are highly concentrated natural fragrances from plant sources that are used in a wide variety of ways: from relaxation, to healing, to improved energy. While each essential oil or blend is used for a different purpose, oils such as peppermint,

lemon, orange, and others offer an energetic pick-me-up. I often wear a necklace diffuser with a blend of those oils in it, and the hint of natural fragrance keeps me energized all day.
- **Give natural stones a try.** If we believe that energy is present in and can connect all things, then it stands to reason that certain natural stones or crystals hold energy that can support and uplift our own energy resources. Some of my favorite go-to jewelry pieces or stones for energy include anything with citrine, ruby, clear quartz, carnelian, and black tourmaline. With so many natural options, feel around until a natural stone chooses you.

Voice

Our difference-making or Soulful Service often asks us to give voice to a cause, to the needs of a population, or to advocate for someone or some outcome. We may be eager for the opportunity to use our voice to contribute to the good of others. Are we as likely and willing to speak up for our own needs and desires? Too often, for too many, the answer is no.

When we feel like we can't or shouldn't have a voice at work, at home, or in the community, it levels a serious blow to our overall sense of well-being. Our voice is important. If we are rusty at using it for our own benefit, it's time to start practicing. Like a muscle, the more we use it, the stronger it gets and the more natural it feels.

- **Speak your truth.** Your opinion counts because it is yours, and you count. If you feel strongly about something, speak up. Even if you don't feel strongly, but you disagree with the prevailing thought, speak up. Even if things don't go our way, we often feel better knowing that we had the courage to speak our truth. Even something as simple as expressing where you would really like to eat

dinner, rather than going with the overused, "I don't care," can be an easy way to practice.
- **Remove the muzzle attached by "what will they think" fears.** This one kept me quiet for years. We can make endless assumptions about how other people might perceive what we have to say. Why do their opinions count any more than our own opinions do? A lot of opinionated people are running around happy to share without giving two craps about what we think. What if we decided that the people who matter will be open to us expressing ourselves and any opinions otherwise are really none of our business?
- **Apply the passion with which you speak up for others to advocating for yourself.** Many Difference Makers are eager to give voice to the people and causes they care about. Imagine if we applied that same willingness to speak up for ourselves.
- **Go public with your voice.** It's a great way to play Big and champion your cause or your own ideas on a broader or deeper scale. Blog. Share live videos. Approach the media for interviews. If you have something to say, there's likely someone out there waiting to hear it. Share your voice.
- **Write privately.** Sometimes giving yourself a voice in the safety of your journal is the place to start. This is great exercise for expressing your feelings, at least to yourself. Finding a friend, family member, or someone else to share these words with can help you become more comfortable about using your voice in progressively bigger ways.
- **Sing!** Even if you suck (like I do), singing is fun and might even make you smile. Not all voice has to be so darn serious. Playing and having fun with our voice can also rejuvenate our energy and uplift our mood.

Resources/Abundance

As a Difference Maker, you may often feel that resources are stretched thin, particularly time and money. There never seems to be enough time to effectively juggle the demands of all your roles, and, whether for your cause or in your bank account, money may feel scarce.

If so, let's upgrade your way of thinking about and interacting with both time and money. When we focus on the money and time we *do have* and all the positive things we are doing with them, then much like in the gratitude exercise, they will seem to increase too. Sure, I get that there are only 24 hours in a day, but what if you got more done in those 24 hours? Or what if the things you were doing were in alignment your goals and priorities? Ahhh ... space to breathe then opens up.

- **Plan for your priorities.** The reason we focus on your values and roles in Part 1 of this book is to really hone in on what your priorities are. When you identify and are really clear about your roles and your values, you can then establish goals and plan your day in a way that ensures progress on those things that matter most to you.
- **Reduce distractions.** Your time is precious. Do you really want to waste big chunks of it on stuff that isn't all that relevant? If part of your self-care routine is binge-watching Netflix or binge Facebooking or gaming or some other thing, simply ask if you are using that to buffer against something you don't really want to face, or if it really matters. If it's super important to you, perhaps make it your reward for finishing up something on your priority goal list.
- **Say "no" and mean it.** "No" is a complete sentence. It's okay to say. If you are asked to do something that is not in alignment with your values or priorities, say no. If you say yes and are resentful about it, you're really not doing anyone any favors.

- **Put time to care for you into your schedule.** Actually put the self-care priorities you choose from this chapter in your calendar. What we schedule has a much greater likelihood of getting done. You are worth it. It's not selfish. In fact, you'll better serve others if you prioritize filling your teapot first.
- **Don't be afraid to look at your finances.** Regardless of how much cash we have, let's not stick our heads in the sand and choose not to look at it. Awareness can be a wonderful thing. This doesn't mean fixating and checking your bank app every hour, but it does mean being willing to be in the know about your own cash flow.
- **View money as energy.** Some Difference Makers attach all kinds of negative stigma to money. Doing so has the effect of repelling it from us. Money is just currency, it's energy. There's nothing inherently good or bad about it. It just is. When you start shifting your thinking about money and welcome it without guilt and negativity, you may just see more of it. Wouldn't that be nice?
- **Make money plans.** We get more out of our time when we manage it. The same is true with money. We can make our resources stretch further and better support our priorities when we are intentional about how we use it.
- **Be willing to invest resources on you.** You are worthy of your own investment. We don't stop investing in our growth and development when that last student loan is taken out. You are the best investment bet you can make. When your tide rises, you lift a bunch of ships with it.

Community/Support

A supportive community can make the difference between progress and failure, between resilience and resistance, between enjoying the journey and just slogging along. In my own experience, when I try to go it alone with whatever the project, the goal, or the situation may be, I'm far less likely to succeed or to enjoy the journey. From the groups I'm in to the clients I coach, I've seen firsthand that accountability, camaraderie, and celebrating success make the journey sweeter and the victory more attainable. And, with a community, if you do happen to stumble and fall, you have others there to either help pick you up or to cheer you on while you pick yourself up. Even we folks with an introvert side need a tribe.

- **Find your tribe.** Find a community of like-minded people where you feel like an insider, not an outsider. Find support and camaraderie. This really matters as you seek to make your difference in a bigger, more authentic, and Love-based way.
- **Engage your family and friends as support.** Be clear with them on what you need to feel supported. And, if they do things that feel like it diminishes support, use your voice to let them know that too.
- **Consider working with a coach.** I chose to enter into coaching because I personally experienced how powerful working with a coach can be. I wanted to be able to contribute to the lives of others through a similar, supportive role. A coach can challenge you, invite you to play bigger, call you on your BS when necessary, and encourage accountability and progress in a way that is hard for most of us to do on our own.
- **Join a group working toward similar goals.** You can find a fantastic sense of shared purpose and focused action when working in a collaborative, group environment with other Difference Makers.

While this list is not intended to be all-encompassing or a huge list of shoulds, it is designed to give you some idea of how you can intentionally enhance the way you show up in each of these eight areas that will help you make an even bigger difference for your cause and your life.

If you are doing something that isn't listed below in these areas, drop me an email at lisa@lisawadeberry.com, and let me know! I keep a running list of client- and reader-submitted ideas, and I would love to know about yours and add it to the online list. Your ideas may be the perfect inspiration for someone else.

SOULFUL SERVICE CONSIDERATIONS:

How many of the ideas are you already doing?
Recognize and celebrate that you are already taking action toward Soulful Self-Care.

In what ways do you believe your difference-making would benefit from your regular practice of some of these ideas?

In thinking about these Eight Spheres of Soulful Self-Care, what specifically will you commit to doing to ensure that your teapot is full?

Who is your tribe? Who specifically can you rely on for encouragement, support, and accountability in pursuit of your goals?

> "You've always had the power my dear, you just had to learn it for yourself."
>
> ~ paraphrased from Glinda the Good Witch from The Wizard of Oz

Part 4: ACTION

SOULFUL SERVICE IS ACTION-ORIENTED:

- Soulful Service requires action. Good intentions are not enough.

- Soulful Service invites you to plan in accordance with your values, strengths, roles, and priorities, then to focus on and fulfill the plan.

- Soulful Service always includes you taking care of you. You are a priority in your own action.

- Soulful Service promotes sustainable action that fills the teapot rather than always leaving it drained dry.

CHAPTER 13

Regularly Bring Real. Big. Love. to Your Life and Service

In my own surveys and interviews with Difference Makers for this book, time and again I heard that they are motivated by their cause and optimistic for a brighter future. I also heard that Difference Makers are often worn out, stressed, hanging on by a thread, and operating in fear of dropping one of the many balls they are juggling.

This was not surprising, given that most people viewed self care as a luxury, not a consistent priority. They assigned guilt to the idea of taking care of themselves, or they put themselves last in priority of all the people and causes that got a proactive chunk of their time. Or, if they did intentionally do things to care for themselves, it was done occasionally, rather than regularly, and most often had to do with their physical body exclusively.

No wonder energy was lagging. All the tending to the growth and well-being of others without regularly watering and weeding their own garden is a recipe for a drought of sustained personal energy.

I raise this out of love, not criticism. If we can keep our teapots full, then not only are we happier and healthier, but we can make a bigger, more sustained difference. If you gain only one takeaway from the time you've invested in this book, then let it be this: self-care is a solid, sustaining foundation for love-based service, not an act of selfishness.

A busy mom of two young daughters, a volunteer, a musician, and a professional, Hillary recognized the social stigma that for too long has accompanied doing what's necessary to support one's own well-being. When asked what advice she has for Difference Makers, Hillary says:

> *"It's not ground breaking or crazy, but it's self-care. We know we need to take care of ourselves, but it's been pooh-poohed for so long. Now we are trying to deprogram ourselves and then teach our kids not to put their needs last. Learn it early. Sometimes I still feel guilty for taking time for me. We have to stay strong in the face of comments that might make us feel guilty. Every decision I make now, I think about what I am modeling for my daughters. We need to learn the value of self-care sooner. We aren't learning it soon enough."*

We know the concept.

"Yeah, yeah, yeah…I get it. Self-love and self-care. Got it."

But do you do it? Some folks are great at this step. The rest of us could use some serious work.

"But you don't understand, I have three kids at home and a business and my volunteer work. I can't fit another thing in."

"But you don't understand. Self-care takes money, which I don't have. So it's not possible for me."

"But you don't understand, taking time for myself means taking time away from my family (job, cause, etc.), and they need me."

"But you don't understand, _____."

Actually, I do understand. I've used every one of those excuses, and dozens more, to try to justify not investing time and energy into my own well-being. I get it. I even took it to an extreme after getting divorced by using service as a way to stay so busy that I didn't have the time, energy, or emotional wherewithal to deal with my own stuff. I stayed focused on those excuses as a way to avoid the pain of dealing with me. My self-soothing at the time was found at the bottom of a Doritos bag, in a six-pack of beer, or after I emptied a pizza box. Yep, been there.

Do you think I was as effective in service as I could have been? Not even close. What I most needed then was self-compassion and self-nurturing. Instead, I threw myself into service and didn't have the focus, the inspiration, the patience, the energy, or the courage that I would have otherwise brought to the table.

I was depleted. My teapot was empty, yet I was still trying to serve from it. In my situation, nothing tragic happened, but I wasn't as able to be fully present, energized or uplifting for others.

However, in some situations, the stakes are much higher, and the importance of proactive self-care is critical.

When Rudy's Alabama National Guard unit responded to the most extensive string of damaging tornadoes in US history, he recognized the toll that sleep deprivation and compassion fatigue could take if those in his unit were not committed to looking out for themselves too.

"Nothing in my life has been more satisfying than playing a role in helping people stabilize and rebuild their lives. I perform a vital function, and my reward is how I feel on the inside at the end of the day," says Rudy.

"We have to take care of ourselves to help others; it's Maslow's Hierarchy in action. If we don't have our stuff together, we can become part of the problem, not the solution. Nobody has ever saved the day by being in bad shape themselves."

Rudy explains that a key leadership principle he learned through service is that people need a reset. For him, that includes wandering, continuous learning, writing in a journal, and occasionally binge-watching SpongeBob.

Coop's reset looks a little different. He unpacks his emotional baggage by taking a solo three- to six-day trek into an Arkansas national forest. He completely unplugs and gets away to reset his mind, his heart, and his perspective. Ultimately, he says, it's an emotional release and a deeply spiritual experience. For a guy who is a self-proclaimed recovering atheist, nature is his sanctuary and the place where he finds a Higher Power.

"By the third day, I literally fall apart, or fall back together, depending on how you look at it," he says. "That's when there's nothing left to do but sit with myself. That's not so easy sometimes. It gets real, then it gets more real. Then, every time, I break down in a 20-minute, gut-wrenching, crying release. It's like a spiritual catharsis. Then the pace slows. It's like—not to sound cheesy—but it's like I'm at one with everything, and I know everything is going to be okay."

For some, the reset might come at the end of a remote, for others it might be going to remote places. The challenge is to find that thing, or that series of things, that help us get back on track or stay on our path.

Fiona invests in personal development, exercising her voice, riding her bike, and having fun offering wine tours at a vineyard near her home.

Hillary makes her mental health a priority. Therapy is a regular part of her monthly schedule, as are exercise, casual meet-ups with good friends and mentors, blogging, and trips to the beach with her daughters.

Sharon commits to regular running to manage the stress of directing programs for CASA (Court Appointed Special Advocate) and to keep her Type 1 diabetes under control.

MaryAnne finds solace in gardening, meditation, reading, and her regular Buddhism learning and practice.

Doug takes a nightly 45-minute walk through his neighborhood to clear his mind, look at the stars, and recharge his batteries.

Do you have a reset when times get tough?

My lack of a regular reset is what prompted my desire to run to a dude ranch in the west and scrub toilets and muck horse stalls to regain perspective.

How are you at tending the garden daily, so the resets don't have to be so dramatic?

This level of self-care doesn't happen by accident. It's planned ... in advance. It's a priority and recognized as necessary for sustainable service to others.

Planning to Bring Real. Big. Love. into Your Life

I love working with clients to get to the heart of what makes their soul sing, taking stock of the roles they play in their life, and then creating a container for their values, their passions, and their vision to take root and really grow. I strive to help clients design a life in which they make their unique difference in a way that nourishes and motivates them, rather than wears them out.

To do so takes some healthy introspection that is, at times, a bit uncomfortable. We identify and shift the unhelpful thought patterns that stand in the way of their success. (For example: Old thought—Self-care is selfish. New Thought—Self-care empowers me to serve in a more energized, sustainable, and enjoyable way.) From a place of clarity and courage, we create a plan designed to bring more joy, energy, and impact to their lives and their difference-making. That, in a nutshell, is what the Real. Big. Love. approach is all about. Getting Real, getting Big (refusing to stay small), and then leading with Love—for yourself and your cause—all according to a well-considered plan.

Plans are funny things. Some of us recoil at the idea of too much structure and specificity and consider them concepts that stifle creativity and suffocate spontaneity. Truth be told, I was once one of those skeptics. Flying by the seat of my pants, ready to take on anything and everything, I ensured that I had plenty of flexibility to tackle other people's priorities and didn't seem quite capable of making progress on the things that really mattered to me.

In 2008, I was introduced to the Best Year Yet® approach to planning, and it literally changed my life for the better. After becoming a trained individual and organizational Best Year Yet® coach, I've used this clear and simple approach to help both individual and nonprofit clients develop smart plans aligned with what matters most to them and that bring accountability into the process.

I've tweaked the goal-setting process a bit to ensure that I take stock in what makes my soul sing. I take a hard look at the previous year to inventory the successes and also note those areas in which I fell short or played small. And I include "Difference Maker" and "Self-Care Champion" goals so these priorities stay in focus.

The months and years that I faithfully create and implement my plan, I stay on track, am able to accomplish so much more that matters to me, and feel energized in the process.

It's when I allow myself to get overwhelmed and choose not to take the time to create or implement a plan, that I feel like I'm running from one obligation to the next, driven by external expectations with my hair on fire. My energy, my health, and my sanity suffer.

Although I once recoiled from personal planning, I now find more freedom in a structured approach to direct my life. It's like the structure creates a container—much like a car—that allows my deepest desires to go somewhere. Rather than spinning my wheels, this planned container gives wheels and a steering wheel and a GPS to my dreams.

For some of us, it takes a mental shift to see the idea of planning from this perspective. But trust me, life, sanity, and service are better for it.

When I work with clients, we map out annual goals that are driven by the roles they play and are anchored in their values. We break them down into quarterly, or 90-day, focus goals. And then build monthly plans to make progress toward the 90-day goals. Most clients then use the monthly plans to help plan their week, and then those weekly plans to drive their daily to-do list. At the end of each month, they take stock in all they've accomplished, analyze what didn't get done and why, and make adjustments as necessary.

This isn't a long, tedious process. It's simply one way to ensure that our most valuable resources, our time and energy, are being wisely invested in the things that really matter in our lives, that keep our teapot full, and that allow us to make the world better through our unique style of Soulful Service.

While many goal-setting and planning systems are available, I've found that building accountability into the process can create the difference between having big dreams and making those dreams a reality. That's what I work with clients to accomplish—to make their Soulful Service manifest in their lives and the world.

Creating a Regular Soulful Self-Care Practice

Guess what! There's no one-size-fits-all magic formula to follow in order to nurture yourself. You get to envision a plan that makes you happy and that you'll actually do regularly.

Sweat~Write~Pray

My Soulful Self-Care practice is to Sweat, Write, and Pray, preferably every day.

Sweat: I've interpreted this to mean any kind of intentional movement or activity in which I have to exert some effort. Running, yoga, strength training, swimming, biking, kayaking, and walking the dog at more than a snail's pace all qualify. I might not sweat per se during yoga or swimming, but it's intentional movement, so it counts.

For me, the intentional movement really has nothing to do with the size of my ass, and everything to do with moving energy through my body. Constipated energy is no bueno. By intentionally moving energy through my system, I find that I make room for more, higher quality energy. Plus, I find that although the movement might relate directly to the physical/body sphere of self-care, it offers positive ripple effects for my mental, emotional, and spiritual spheres as well. And, if I'm moving with family or friends, add the community component in too.

Write: I journal. A lot. I have for years. When I journal, it's not about pouring all my secrets into a locked diary. Rather, I use the page to clear out any stuck emotions or thoughts, to capture big ideas and opportunities, and then to invite the guidance and support of Spirit.

To me, journaling is a highly spiritual activity. I intentionally turn off the inner critic of the Bully Brain, open my heart, and seek to access the wisdom that Spirit may be inclined to share with me on that day. The guidance and encouragement is always upbeat, positive, supportive, and loving. The guidance is offered in such a way as to help me align with my soul and my purpose, and to courageously move in that direction.

The idea for the Real. Big. Love. coaching program and this book came through one of these journaling sessions. The encouragement for Sweat~Write~Pray came through one of these journaling sessions.

Making it a priority each day to connect with my journal improves my life. It's that simple. Even five minutes in the morning helps set the day on a more positive, productive, and purposeful course.

The act of writing is a tool I use for emotional self-care, but it also invokes spiritual connection, helps clear mental clutter, and frees my voice. Sometimes I share my writings with an online community (check out Soulful Musings with a Side of Sass on Facebook). Again, it's one practice that benefits multiple spheres of self-care.

Pray: Prayer looks and feels different for every person. There's no one right way to pray. To me, this simply means connecting and communicating with Spirit, in whatever way that may look to you.

Sometimes I talk with the Divine. I give thanks. I am in awe. I ask for help. Other times, I clear my mind so Spirit can talk to me. That's the nature of meditation, and I include it under the banner of "pray."

Some of my best, most focused prayer happens when I run. Granted, in the beginning it was, "God, please don't let me fall down or pass out. God, please keep my heart beating and my lungs breathing." As my running has gotten a bit easier, my prayers have shifted too. This is one way that I can feed my body and my soul at the same time, by praying while doing something else.

I often pray during commutes, while in the shower, or before drifting off to sleep. I don't employ a standard prayer format or ritualized system of prayer, although that can be super helpful and inspiring to some. I simply talk and also listen.

Obviously, this sits squarely in the spiritual sphere of self-care. I've also found that prayer improves my mental outlook and my emotional well-being, helps me find words and courage to exercise my voice, and offers built-in community by connecting to the Divine.

Taken together, Sweat~Write~Pray dramatically improves both the quantity and quality of my energy. I feel better, I think clearer, my heart is lighter, and I feel connected to my bigger sense of purpose. And I'm nicer to be around. If I haven't engaged my practice for a while, my family is quick to pick up on it because I tend to get pretty cranky.

Sweat~Write~Pray is my regular go-to practice. In addition, I seek to regularly "grow my brain" through classes and workshops. I work with coaches and coaching groups for community, inspiration, and accountability. And I enjoy adventures in nature with family as much as I can. This is how I keep my teapot full.

Integral Transformative Practice

Integral Transformative Practice (ITP) is a personal growth practice that integrates body, mind, heart, and soul. Developed in 1992 through a two-year experimental group class in human transformation, the practice combines physical movement, creative visualization and affirmations, and meditation.

The ITP practice includes a series of physical movements called a kata that are accessible to nearly anyone. The intent is to move energy through the body while articulating nearly all the major joints. It is both relaxing and energizing, drawing on elements from aikido, yoga, tai chi, and other practices.

Serious ITP practitioners also follow the nine ITP Commitments. These Commitments hit on all eight spheres of Soulful Self-Care. They include taking personal responsibility for progress, seeking community, physical movement, being conscious of nutrition, growing intellectually, opening the heart to love and being of service, expressing feelings, and meaningful affirmations. The goal behind ITP is to offer a research-supported path of practice and a supportive community to help us take personal responsibility in exploring and expanding how we envision and express our own potential. Pretty powerful stuff.

I had the opportunity to participate in a four-month "Mastery in the Heartland" ITP program. I learned that the practice truly can be life-affirming and life-improving. It was through this program and community that I found the courage to write this book as part of my own version of Soulful Service.

More information about ITP is available at the nonprofit organization's website, www.itp-international.org, and also through the book *The Life We are Given* by Michael Murphy and George Leonard.

Create Your Own Practice

While Sweat~Write~Pray and Integral Transformative Practice are two Soulful Self-Care practices that I've found to be helpful, they may not be for you, and that's completely okay. The key is to find a path of Soulful Self-Care that meets your needs and your interests, and that you will actually commit to and do.

You completed the Self-Care assessment and determined where your biggest opportunities exist. You even picked a couple of ideas from different self-care spheres to commit to. Now own them. Make them part of your regular routine. Put them in your calendar. Put reminders on your phone. Do whatever it takes to honor yourself enough to make taking care of you in a meaningful way a priority in your life.

Over time, your needs and focus may change as you grow and change. That's to be expected. If you are taking stock of your needs and accomplishments at least annually, preferably more often, you'll know when it's time to shift and mix it up.

Don't for a second believe that you are not worth the time investment or that it's selfish to plan and prioritize you. Trust me when I say that the way you show up in the world and the service you are able to offer to your family, your cause, and your community, will benefit when you make you a priority. Only then can you engage in inspired, sustainable, meaningful Soulful Service.

SOULFUL SERVICE CONSIDERATIONS:

What is your current Soulful Self-Care practice?

How would your difference-making benefit by you making Self-Care a regular habit?

Do you currently plan your years, months, weeks, or days? Do your priorities drive your plans?

Would having outside accountability help you better stick to your plans and achieve your goals?

Chapter 14

Obstacles to Serving and Living with Real. Big. Love.

We started this journey learning about Kris—a go-getting Difference Maker who frequently found herself exhausted, overwhelmed, and feeling the sting of all the self-inflicted "shoulds" she didn't have time enough in the day to accomplish.

I feel like I've walked a marathon or two in Kris's uncomfortable shoes. How about you?

When Kris and I first met, she had two things working against her that tended to make the wounds of all those undone "shoulds" that much more painful.

First, her expectations of what she could accomplish in a day were sorely unrealistic. Her daily to-do list often contained 30 or more items, many of which would take an hour or more to reasonably complete. She set herself up for failure before she even got going by expecting far too much out of herself and allowing others to expect it out of her too. Her pace and performance were unsustainable, her energy was bolstered by massive amounts of caffeine and chocolate, and all she really wanted was a night of good, unworried sleep, which of course never happened.

Second, she recognized the need to better care for herself but would consistently put her own well-being on the backburner to attend to that growing list of unmanageable to-dos. As her weight and blood pressure increased and her sleep quality grew even worse, she would make plans to turn things around. The latest new diet or plan to go to the gym would start off with a bang, until a big deadline, a sick child, or marital stress won her attention, time, and energy again.

The more things fell apart, the more Kris would bury herself in busyness as a way to escape. Her life became a spiraling mess of other people's priorities and her own unmet needs, making her dizzy with self-doubt, frustration, and confusion about how to get on a more sane and sustainable path.

Through our work together, Kris first gained clarity on what was really important to her and how she could make her own unique contribution in the world. Kris got Real, and in doing so recognized the need to let go of the commitments, the expectations, and the busyness that were ill-aligned with her new-found clarity.

Next Kris identified opportunities to show up in a more courageous, more consistent, and more effective way for what was important to her. Kris got Big. In doing so, she began to appreciate the value of taking both big steps to support her cause, and also smaller daily steps to support her own well-being. Kris quit quitting on the things that brought her joy and vitality.

Then Kris identified areas in her life where fear, not love, had been in the captain's seat and steering her ship. She met this recognition with quick and honest commitments to stop allowing her fears to throw her dreams and her vitality overboard.

As could be predicted, Kris made great progress in the dreaming phase. She was great at talking a good game at the outset of any potential big shift. She legitimately did get excited and saw the possibilities, and she knew that life could be different, could feel better.

Then the resistance set in.

Kris is a smart woman. The number of rational-sounding, well-meaning objections to actually changing anything was quite impressive. The fear reared up, and her mind was actively at work creating fascinating horror stories about all the things that could go wrong if she actually did crazy things like say no, put less on the daily to-do list, acted from the edge of her comfort zone, and prioritized being kind, compassionate, and loving to herself.

She convinced herself, through the clever musings of her mind, that her world would fall apart.

So we went to work unraveling these tangled mental tales that felt more like a noose than a friendly warning from fear.

Anytime we set out to step into and live from a bolder, more aligned and more authentic version of ourselves, we will face opposition and obstacles. It's inevitable.

I break these obstacles into three categories: Self, Others, and the Universe.

Standing in Your Own Way

It turns out we really are our own biggest pains in the ass. Even when making progress, even with a plan laid out, even with volume control on the Bully Brain, we have the amazing capacity to upend our own success. When our mind runs amok, we create elaborate tales predicting terrible fates, we doubt ourselves, we worry, and we question our right to say or do whatever it is we want to say or do. Ultimately, we are at risk of tripping up our own progress and letting ourselves down ... again.

We revert back to those four-letter F-bombs that seem intent on effing up our progress. Hello, old frenemies, Fear, Fail, and Fine. You've shown up again. Even when we think we've mustered the Faith, the Fortitude, and the Fullness to push beyond these little buggers, they come up again and again, in ways big and small, to test our resolve.

How bad do you want this? How important is this mission? Oh, you think you are going to invest in you today, do you? Who do you think you are to do x, y, z? Oh wow, are "they" ever going to hate you. You're not skinny enough, good-looking enough, strong enough, rich enough, smart enough.... What are you going to tell people when you fail again this time? Haven't you learned your lesson by now?

This can be hard. And sometimes we fall. Sometimes we give up. Sometimes we taste a hint of opposition, and we run for the hills.

A crying baby, a depleted bank account, an exhausted body, and lack of support may look like quicksand to even the most well-meaning dreams, but that was the cauldron in which J.K. Rowling conjured Harry Potter. Our struggles will happen, and we can choose to allow them to bury us, or we can choose for that to be the very fertilizer that helps us grow.

Letting Others Steer Your Ship

I'll admit, I've invested an awful lot of energy over the decades worrying about what other people might think. With every word I write, every speech I give, every class I teach, or every workshop I lead, I could easily tone everything down to alleviate any possibility of being offensive. Often, we want to make a difference that will contribute to the happiness of others, so the thought of inspiring their judgment instead of their growth or their thanks, can be a disincentive to being Real, Big, or Love-directed.

Sometimes, it's the well-meaning people closest to you who try to pull you off your path. They may genuinely care about your well-being, your feelings, the state of your relationships, or your personal safety. They may believe that being authentic and bold is dangerous and scary. They want you to live their version of what is "best" for you.

Or maybe they are concerned that, if you grow, if you change, if you step into your Real, Big, Loving, beautiful self, they will no longer have a place in your life. They may try to keep you small so you don't outgrow them.

Others can also want their priorities to be your priorities. As you begin to focus more of your energy and time in those things that support your values, and that are true to the difference you want to make, you will begin to say no to the requests and personal agendas of others. Some people don't like to hear no and will let you know about it. When you allow the priorities of others to take precedence over your own, you are effectively saying no to yourself and to your own Soulful Service.

We can also pre-emptively and negatively judge the possible reactions of others and use that to justify inaction. Living in the Bible Belt, I look back at all the times I've wanted to leap out and add my voice to the world and stopped myself with the simple thought, "What would the Baptists think?" Today, I can write this while smiling, but not so long ago it created a serious block for me.

Do you really want to hand others that much power over your life?

It's time to reclaim being the captain of your own ship.

Roadblocks from the Universe

"Follow your bliss and the universe will open doors where there were only walls," advised Joseph Campbell, the man who taught us the unifying power of mythology. Yet it is in following our bliss that we may come to encounter those walls in the first place. His encouragement is to not give up, follow the bliss more, and watch as transformation happens.

Throughout his writings about the Hero's Journey, Campbell notes that great myths and great adventures include what he calls a "Threshold Guardian." This can be a person, a thing, or a predicament that tests our resolve.

You have a big deadline, and your computer crashes. Do you give up, or do you find a workaround? You get a flat tire on the way to an important meeting. Do you throw in the tire iron and call it a day, or do you keep charging forward? You go to sign a lease on the perfect office space and find out it is no longer available. You get back into the dating game after years on the sidelines and quickly find plenty of toads and no princes. You finally launch a new book or program or idea, and it's a total flop.

In each of these situations, something happened that could have pulled you off your path, made you question your direction, or prompted you to fully retreat. In each instance, you have a choice. Keep trying, or tuck tail and run.

Roadblocks might demand an alternate route, an alternate mode of transportation, or even some help to get around. But they don't have to be deal-breakers or dream-crushers. Once you show the Threshold Guardians that you are serious and that you are not backing down, walls of opposition can become doors of opportunity.

Obstacles happen. If you are not facing obstacles of some sort, then your aim is too low. Meaningful potential and progress pave the way for obstacles. They also pave the way for making your greatest contribution and leaving the world a better place. The choice is ultimately up to you.

As Joseph Campbell also said, "Opportunities to find deeper powers within ourselves come when life seems most challenging."

Will you let the challenges get in your way and keep you small, or will you use them as the fuel to get on with making your Soulful difference with Real. Big. Love?

What obstacles can you expect? What's your plan for dealing with them? How will you stay on course even when things get hard?

Once I made the decision to finally write this book and invested in a program to help me, the Threshold Guardians decided to work overtime testing my resolve.

The day after I took out a loan to invest in a pricey writing program, my husband lost his job and the family's health insurance. Although I was working in my own business, book-writing needed to take a backseat so I could quickly find a job with health insurance. In addition to coaching, consulting, and writing, I became a full-time college political science instructor. My attention shifted.

The next month, a family member got into legal trouble, spent three nights in the county jail, and needed financial and moral support to get through. That resulted in a huge stress reaction in our home.

I took on additional adjunct teaching jobs to help make ends meet, which meant even less time for writing.

Next, I caught a bad case of the flu, and then lingering bronchitis, and faced some injuries that put the running part of my self-care plan on hold.

Through all this I was still trudging along on the book, but progress wasn't happening as I had hoped, and giving up was not an option.

After seven months of unemployment, my husband started a new job, only to discover another hostile boss and unscrupulous work environment. This lead to him facing massive anxiety, panic attacks, and depression. After three months, he was recruited to join another company, which decided to cut the new position after only two weeks. He's unemployed again, and finances are scary.

At the same time, my dad got sick. Really sick. He spent eight weeks in the hospital, 20 days of which were in intensive care. I was the only relative within a five-hour drive who could consistently help and regularly visit him. Given the severity of his situation, we nearly lost him more than once. Making end-of-life plans for a parent is never easy. Even the doctors are surprised he made it.

Then, two hours away from sending a rewrite of this book to my new editor, my hard drive completely crashed—unrecoverable—and I hadn't saved the edited files anywhere else. (PSA for the day: Back up early and often.)

Obstacles. Check.

It's as if the Universe was testing to make sure I was really serious this time about completing a book. I'd started others; I'd finished none. The Universe was making sure I walked the talk of the book. Even in difficult circumstances that hit right at home, could I make progress on my priorities, serve with Real. Big. Love, and commit to my self-care?

Honestly, it wasn't easy. Of course, it could have been harder. I'm not looking for a pity party or trying to complain. It's simply that I thought I had created the perfect time to commit to a big goal, then stuff got nuts.

But now you are reading this, which means despite the delays and the challenges, I didn't give up.

The past year has been trying. I had to change things up a bit. I had to double-down on my self-care routine for the sake of my sanity and overall health. It didn't keep me from getting the flu, but it kept me from losing my spark.

I had to reprioritize where I invested my time, energy, and money.

And, although financially some would argue it made little sense, it was when situations were most challenging that I knew I had to invest in a coaching program. When the chips were down, I knew that betting on myself was the best investment I could make to turn things around, to grow, and to step even more into a vision of Real. Big. Love. for my life and service. I needed the support, the encouragement, the accountability, and the opportunity to voice my fears and reframe them. I needed an outside perspective to help me keep moving forward.

Thanks to all the obstacles that mounted, and with the insight of my coach, I realized that the guaranteed income from my faculty job at the college didn't come close to meeting the financial needs of my family. Playing it safe wasn't paying the bills, and I knew I needed to step into a Bigger version of service and re-commit to my business and attracting new clients. Plus, that's what makes my soul sing.

Every client I work with faces obstacles and challenges. It's simply the human experience of growth and meaningful progress. Together, we align back with what is Real, focus on Faith over Fear, identify those opportunities to lead with Love, and then ensure that the action is happening to make their brand of Soulful Service alive in the world.

I needed a coach to keep moving forward. My clients benefit from coaching to help them move forward. Perhaps working with a coach could also help you step over obstacles and step into an even bolder, more vibrant version of Real. Big. Love. for your service and your life.

If so, let's talk.

SOULFUL SERVICE CONSIDERATIONS:

What obstacles can you envision tripping up your plans,
your self-care, or your service?

Are you aware of how you might get in your own way
to prevent progress toward living and serving
from a more inspired, sustainable, and meaningful way?

How supportive are the people in your life of your growth?
Are they helpful or a hinderance to your efforts
to live and serve with Real. Big. Love?

How could working with a coach support you
in stepping into the next, more inspired version
of your life and your service?

Conclusion

This world, now more than ever it seems, needs inspired, soulful Difference Makers committed to investing our unique gifts, energy, courage, and love into the causes that light up our hearts and make a meaningful contribution to the world.

The path of Soulful Service is not necessarily easy. It can be fraught with challenges and obstacles. It can make you question your courage and your own resolve. But when you are committed to serving from a place of soulfulness, your *why* shines like a beacon to push the shadows of doubt aside and light your way forward.

Through this book, and through the very idea of Soulful Service, I'm inviting you to grow. Growth can be scary, yet it is necessary to offer your bolder, more authentic action on behalf of your service and in your life.

How you treat yourself often is reflected in how you interact with others.

Think about that for a minute.

To soulfully serve others, you need a spot on your own priority list. That means being willing to do the sometimes difficult introspection that helps you get clear about your why, about your values, Inner Gifts and the roles you want to play in your life. This is how you get Real. Being Real brings the very best of yourself to benefit your service.

To soulfully serve others, you need to be willing to break through your own comfort zones to play Big in your commitment. This will take courage. This will take consistency. The difference you want to make and the value you want to bring deserve nothing less.

To soulfully serve others, you need to be willing to lead with Love. That means holding space for unconditional love with others, especially when it is challenging, by recognizing that Namaste quality in each of us. It also means loving yourself enough to steer your own ship, keep your own teapot full, and to facilitate the support you need to live into a bigger, more authentic version of yourself and your service.

The stories throughout this book depict regular people working to make a real difference. They've faced exhaustion and frustration. They've faced enormous service-related highs and heartbreaking lows. Some recognized the value of self-care from the beginning and built it into their routine. Others faced hardships or difficult diagnoses before they made themselves and their own well-being a priority.

Your difference-making will shift and evolve over time. That's to be expected. During the course of writing this book, with the challenges that took place in my own life, I had to shift my focus. I gave up volunteer community development efforts and sitting on nonprofit boards of organizations I cared about in order to focus my energy on teaching, caring for my dad, offering moral support to my husband, and writing. It's all still service, it simply looks different now. It took me a while to recognize that was okay, that I wasn't turning my back on my community, but rather turning my attention toward my family, students, clients, and future readers.

The Eight Spheres of Soulful Self-Care help me and my clients stay on track, especially when the going gets tough. My hope is that in creating a meaningful and regular self-care practice, you will derive the benefits so that your greater contribution can be driven by a full teapot. May your service be uplifting and sustainable.

Too many Difference Makers try to go it alone and shy away from asking for or receiving help. Please know this does you and those you serve no favors, and it denies the opportunity for others to be of service to you. You will need help sometimes. You are worthy of it. It will ultimately help you serve even better.

It is with sincere appreciation that I thank you for the contribution you make in your family, your organization, for your cause, in your community—in this world. It matters.

I've developed individual and group coaching programs to promote Soulful Service and support Difference Makers in bringing Real. Big. Love. to their cause and their life. This community supports and encourages Difference Makers to look deep within themselves in order to discover their own inner treasure and then share that with the world in a Big and Love-filled way. It offers loving, insightful guidance, and the accountability and mindset check to help members really show up for their cause and their life. I've also developed a program specifically for Difference Making organizations to help foster Real. Big. Love. in the organizational culture and even in strategic planning with purpose. If you'd like to learn more about this aspect of the work, please visit www.lisawadeberry.com/RealBigLove.

Those you serve need you. You need you. Let's all be here for each other to support more Soulful Service in the world.

Real. Big. Love. to you.

Resources

Take Time for Your Life: A Personal Coach's 7-Step Program for Creating the Life You Want, Cheryl Richardson, 1999.

The Big Leap: Conquer Your Hidden Fear and Take Life to the Next Level, Gay Hendrix, 2010.

What Matters Most: The Power of Living Your Values, Hyrum Smith, 2001.

You are a Badass: How to Stop Doubting Your Greatness and Start Living an Awesome Life, Jen Sincero, 2013.

The Gifts of Imperfection: Let Go of Who You Think You're Supposed to Be and Embrace Who You Are, Brené Brown, 2010.

The Life We are Given: A Long-Term Program for Realizing the Potential of Boy, Mind, Heart, and Soul, Michael Murphy and George Leonard, 1995.

Un-Settling: How to Help Your Kids by Making and Modeling an Amazing Life After Divorce, Maggie McReynolds, 2018.

The Healthy, Happy Nonprofit: Strategies for Impact without Burnout, Beth Kanter and Aliza Sherman, 2016.

Your Best Year Yet! Ten Questions for Making the Next Twelve Months Your Most Successful Ever, Jenni Ditzler, 2000. (www.bestyearyet.com)

Integral Transformative Practice, www.itp-international.org

Acknowledgements

Writing this first book is a dream far too many years in the making. I am incredibly grateful for the inspiration and support, both directly and indirectly, of those who played a role in helping me conceive, nurture, and finally birth this book baby.

Most importantly, I would like to acknowledge all the people in this world striving to make a positive difference for people, for causes, and for the planet. I especially appreciate those who shared your stories and experience to inform the book and make it richer. I can't imagine a world void of people like you seeking to lift up others and serving from a place of compassion and optimism. I am grateful to each of you for contributing in your own unique way. May our paths cross in the future, and may we continue to make our difference from a place of Real. Big. Love.

To my daughter Riley, who is my biggest teacher and my greatest inspiration, thank you for making this world a brighter, kinder place and for giving me the honor of being your mom.

To my husband Jeremy, for showing me love, support, strength, and encouragement more beautiful than I could have ever imagined. I love we.

To my mom Charlotte Wade, for giving me roots and encouraging my wings. If I fly, it's thanks to you.

This book would still be a dream rather than a reality without the support, loving guidance, and accountability of my editor and writing coach, Maggie McReynolds, and the team at Un-Settling Books. I deeply and genuinely appreciate you.

It is with great appreciation that I acknowledge the coaches and tribes that I've grown with over the years.

To the Juicy Girls—Maggie, Marcy, and Ruth—Big Love was born with you, and with your help, the Real came about, too. I have big love for all y'all.

To my fellow pilgrims in the Osage Forest of Peace School for Spiritual Direction, I appreciate your insight and support as we grow together on this journey of deeper understanding.

To my coach Tamara Arnold and the lovely souls in the Chakra Business Academy and Magical Mastermind. Thank you. Deeply and sincerely. We are all magic in the making, and you helped me to realize that about myself too.

Bob Doenges, I believe our meeting was by Divine arrangement, and for that I am eternally grateful. Thank you for showing me the beauty in being a "servant of servants," for teaching me that "grace is in the receiving," for re-igniting my love of poetry, and for introducing me to ITP and its family. You've made an indelible impression on my life, and I am deeply appreciative.

And, Dad … thank you for helping me, in your own way, learn some of the hardest, yet most important lessons in this life. It hasn't always been easy, but I am stronger and more compassionate because I've had the chance to share this life with you.

About the Author

LISA WADE BERRY

Like those she serves, Lisa Wade Berry simply wants to help make the world a better place. Through smart, inspired communication, management, and advocacy strategies and personal empowerment coaching, she helps promote positive change from the inside out.

Lisa's broad-based experience includes providing media and communication strategies, program development, facilitation, strategic planning and leadership to national and local nonprofits, political and advocacy campaigns, the film industry, members of Congress, schools, government agencies, businesses, athletes, and recording artists. She also teaches college political science, speech, and business classes, including inside two state correctional centers. A community activist at heart, Lisa has served on numerous boards to promote arts, education, and enhanced quality of life.

Lisa earned bachelor's degrees in communication and public relations from William Jewell College in Liberty, MO, and a master's degree from the Graduate School of Political Management at George Washington University in Washington, D.C. For her graduate studies, she received the Henry D. Paley award given to the valedictorian of each graduating class.

Lisa enjoys learning about the spiritual beliefs of ancient cultures, believes that love and energy are the keys to unlock greater potential, and would rather be on a river than just about anywhere else. She is an enthusiastic, back-of-the-pack half marathon runner and the alpha-wannabe to a pack of goofy, lovable dogs. Lisa lives with her husband Jeremy and daughter Riley in a small community in eastern Oklahoma where the people are friendly and the sky is huge.

Thank You

Thank you for the work you do to make a positive difference in this world. And thank you for reading Real. Big. Love. and incorporating the tenets of Soulful Service. I would love the chance to stay connected with you and better serve your unique and specific needs. Here are some ways we can do that:

1. NEWSLETTER: Sign up to receive my newsletter. You will receive the latest news about Real. Big. Love. workshops, coaching, and other projects I have in the works, as well as new and timely ideas and encouragement to promote Soulful Service in action. Join here: http://lisawadeberry.com/contact/getnews/

2. REVIEW: Write a Review! If this book offered an idea or encouragement that could be useful to you and your service, please let others know. Please consider leaving a review on Amazon or the website of your favorite bookseller.
I appreciate you!

3. CONSULTING/SPEAKING: If your cause could benefit from incorporating the ideas of Real. Big. Love. and the art of Soulful Service into its organizational culture, I would love to help. Contact me at lisa@lisawadeberry.com to discuss how to apply these concepts to your unique mission and culture within your organization.

4. LET'S TALK! How would you like a free conversation about how to amplify the Soulfulness of your service and bring more Real. Big. Love. to your cause and life? Be one of the first 100 readers to sign up for a free, 30-minute Soulful Service Amp Up conversation with me. You can schedule your appointment here: http://lisawadeberry.com/contact/schedulesession.

5. CONNECT: In addition to the newsletter, we can stay connected in real-time through social media. You can find me on Facebook @lisawadeberryauthor, on Instagram @lisawadeberry and on LinkedIn, www.linkedin.com/in/lisawadeberry.

www.ingramcontent.com/pod-product-compliance
Lightning Source LLC
Chambersburg PA
CBHW071207070526
44584CB00019B/2950